Josie

A Memoir

by

Joe Edd Morris

Copyright © Joe Edd Morris

All rights reserved. No part of this publication may be reproduced, distributed, or transmitted in any form or by any means, including photocopying, recording, or other electronic or mechanical methods, without the prior written permission of the publisher, except in the case of brief quotations embodied in critical reviews and certain other noncommercial uses permitted by copyright law.

ISBN-978-1-951300-66-1

Liberation's Publishing LLC
West Point - Mississippi

Also by Joe Edd Morris

FICTION

Land Where My Fathers Died

The Prison

Torched: Summer of '64

The Lost Page

The Lost Gospel

NON-FICTION

Ten Things I Wish Jesus Hadn't Said

Old Testament Stories: What Do They Say Today?

New Testament Stories: What Do They Say Today?

Revival of the Gnostic Heresy: Fundamentalism

The Christian Right: Neither Christian nor Right

Jury Selection in Mississippi: A Systematic Approach

Joe Edd Morris

Contents

Chapter 1: Genes 3

Chapter 2: Josie's Parents 7

Chapter 3: First Home 23

Chapter 4: Early School Years 31

Chapter 5: College Days and First Job 41

Chapter 6: The Watchmaker 55

Chapter 7: The War Years 65

Chapter 8: The Jewelry Store 69

Chapter 9: The Entrepreneur 73

Chapter 10: The Businesswoman 79

Chapter 11: Renaissance Woman 89

Chapter 12: Brown v Board of Education 95

Chapter 13: Traveling Josie 105

Chapter 14: Sarge 123

Chapter 15: Sarge with a Heart 137

Chapter 16: The Long Arm of Josie 145

Chapter 17: The Second Bill 157

Chapter 18: Last Days 167

Chapter 19: Eulogy 183

Chapter 20: Epilogue 187

Appendix A: Ferguson Siblings Bios 191

Appendix B: Growing Up on Marshall Hill 211

Appendix C: Depression Days 1929-1932 215

Appendix D: Josie's Reunion Letter to Classmates 243

Appendix E: Susie Bell's Favorite Recipes 245

Appendix F: Suzie Belle Ferguson Eulogy 247

Acknowledgements 249

To David

And

To Jimmie

In Memory of William Edward "Bill" Morris and William "Bill" Devan Blizzard

And Josie's closest friends—Inez, Jamie, Mabel, Bess Ann, Pearl, Helen, Odie, M. J., and Jackie

Everyone wants to write a book about their mother. Why did I choose to write one about mine? Why should you want to read it?

Have you ever met a woman—

Who was Annie Oakley, Scarlet O'Hara, Molly Brown, Harriet Tubman, and Eleanor Roosevelt all rolled into one?

Who, on a Sunday morning, faced down desperadoes on a saloon porch in Jackson Hole, Wyoming?

Who could out-barter, out-haggle, and out-dicker a conman?

Who, single-handedly, and briefly, controlled traffic in downtown Chicago so her husband could back out of a parking space?

Whose beauty and charm attracted suitors from the highest ranks of politics, power, and wealth, yet she preferred a gentle and humble watchmaker?

Who was an entrepreneurial, self-taught interior designer and gemologist and transformed that husband's watch repair shop into a dazzling emporium of jewels, fine China and crystal ... and flowers ... and hats ... and pianos ... and antiques?

Who, after her husband's death, continued to support and care for his ex-wife in a Tennessee sanitarium?

Who staged a one-woman campaign to bring racial justice and equal opportunity to Mississippi in the '50's and 60's?

Who was a Renaissance woman—artist, musician, singer, dancer?

May I introduce to you my mother, Joan "Josie" Ferguson Morris.

Figure 1. Josie Christmas 2003

Chapter 1: Genes

With the interpretation of any text, biblical or otherwise, context is essential. The same is true of understanding and interpreting a life, a personality, a character. Background, milieu, and circumstances are indispensable.

In the late 1600s and early 1700s, escalating rents and hard times drove thousands of persons from Scotland and the Celtic borderlands of England to America. Nineteen out of twenty immigrants were farmers. One group of families came from Perth, Scotland. They settled first in Maryland and Virginia, migrated through North and South Carolina, across Alabama, and into middle Tennessee where new Indian Territory had opened for settlers. From LaGrange and Chapel Hill, Tennessee (Hardeman County), a group moved into what is now Union County, Mississippi and settled in a place called Rocky Ford, near the Salem Methodist Church just east of the Enterprise community.

They were hardy adventurers, tough, stubborn, and fiercely independent. They were competitive entrepreneurs, intelligent, bright, and outspoken.

They were the Fergusons.

Ansel Ferguson, Josie's great-great grandfather, was the son of James Ferguson and Elizabeth (Betsy) Fleming Ferguson who migrated to the colonies from Scotland around 1785. Born March 31, 1800 Ansel married Nancy Cynthia Foster on February 1, 1824 in Greene County, Alabama, southwest of Tuscaloosa. Around 1826, Ansel and Nancy Cynthia moved from Alabama to LaGrange, Tennessee,

Hardeman County, where most of their nine children were born. Ansel raised racehorses and was known for entering them in competitions throughout western Tennessee.

On May 24, 1834, Ansel witnessed the Treaty of Pontotoc Creek between the Chickasaw Nation, represented by Chief Ish-ta-ho-te-pa, and the U. S. Government. Chickasaw Indian land was then opened for settlers. In 1846, Ansel bought his first land in Mississippi in what is now Union County near the Poolville community. Fourteen years later, in 1860, he bought a section of land in the Mt. Pisgah community. Today, Mt. Pisgah is located off state Highway 30 on County Road 27 about halfway between New Albany, the county seat, and Darden Lake. Ansel and his family finally settled near the Salem and Rocky Ford communities. At some point, Ansel donated and deeded a two-acre plot to be used for the Mt. Pisgah cemetery. He died on July 7, 1881. Nancy Cynthia's death followed in December of 1886. Both are buried in the Mt. Pisgah cemetery.

Samuel Harrison Ferguson, son of Ansel and Nancy Cynthia, and Josie's grandfather, was born October 26, 1826, in LaGrange, Tennessee. On March 6, 1859, presumably at the Salem Methodist Church, he married Martha Ann Gilliam. Samuel and Martha Ann are also buried in the Mt. Pisgah cemetery.

Samuel and Nancy Cynthia had eight children. One was Josie's father, John Gilliam "Jake" Ferguson. He was born "after the Surrender" in 1869, in Galway, a small community near Mt. Pisgah, Rocky Ford and Salem, Mississippi.

French Hugenots began coming to the American Colonies in the 1600s. Pursuing religious freedom and fleeing taxes and persecution, they migrated from northern France through Ireland. They settled initially in North and South Carolina, then migrated across Alabama and into what is now Union County, Mississippi, and settled in the Salem community.

They were hardy adventurers, tough, stubborn, and fiercely independent. Intelligent, bright, and outspoken. They, too, were competitive entrepreneurs.

They were the Lamars.

Thomas Lamar, Josie's great-great grandfather, was born 1774 and around 1795-96, he married Mary (last name unknown). Their son, Josie's great grandfather, Thomas Fletcher Lamar, was born in 1799 and married Mary Ellis on January 8, 1829. The last of their six children, John Harris Lamar, was born about 1849 and on January 28, 1864, he married Susie Ann Morris. Their ninth child, Susie Belle, was born on March 9, 1873. She was Josie's mother.

The Fergusons and Lamars lived in the small community of Rocky Ford. They attended the same church, traveled the same paths, and shopped in the same general store. At some point in the early 1890s, at a church dinner-on-the-grounds or a revival or in passing at the general store, twenty-five-year-old John Gilliam "Jake" Ferguson laid eyes on twenty-one-year-old Susie Belle Lamar and on September 13, 1894, they were married in the Salem Methodist Church.

The Salem Methodist Church dates back to 1840 when it was organized, and that section of the state was part of the Memphis Annual Conference. It later became part of the North Mississippi Conference. While a student at Ole Miss, I served as the pastor of the Oxford Methodist Circuit and had the opportunity of preaching in the church where my grandparents had been members and were married.

At the time of their marriage, the church was a single room, dirt floor, log dwelling. Split logs on pegged legs served as seats. The windows were flanked by wooden shutters. Parishioners arrived for services in ox wagons, or they walked. According to records provided by The History of Union County 1989, one of the charter members and an early song leader was Thomas Lamar, grandfather of Susie Belle Lamar.

Following their marriage, Jake and Susie Belle moved in with his parents, Samuel Harrison, and Martha Gilliam Ferguson. In her memoirs, Blanche Ferguson Aldrich, Josie's older sister, described her grandparents' house in her chronicles of those early times:

> The home place was a painted house very rare in the post-bellum days. It had lightning rods, which added prestige, and the cookhouse was a few feet away from the main house. There was a walk from the cookhouse to the house. Grandmama kept the kitchen floor clean with sand and lye soap which she made. The house had an ash barrel below the roof valleys. There was a hole at the bottom and a container there to catch the lye as it seeped through. This was used with the grease saved from the kitchen to make the soap. Grandmama's floors were white and safe to eat off.

After the birth of their first child Guy, Jake and Susie Belle left Samuel Harrison and Martha Gilliam's home and moved to a log house with two rooms, a dogtrot between them and a lean-to kitchen. In that austere and primitive environment, they began their family.

Chapter 2: Josie's Parents

James Gilliam "Jake" Ferguson was born September 29, 1869.

That year, Ulysses S. Grant was sworn in as the 18th President of the United States. The Reconstruction era and Gilded Age were in full swing. The Golden Spike was driven, marking the completion of the first Transcontinental Railroad. Jesse James robbed his first bank. The first intercollegiate game of football was played—Rutgers v. Princeton. The first plastic celluloid was patented, and the Cincinnati Red Stockings opened the baseball season as the first fully professional baseball team.

Biographical information on Jake Ferguson is scarce. The youngest of eight, he was born four years "after the Surrender." Because little education was available during the Civil War, he received more than his siblings. After the War, terms in the best schools lasted only four months. Jake once remarked to his daughter Blanche, "If all of my months of schooling were added up, I'd have a fourth-grade education." He would go on to achieve educational accomplishments for his family and for his community, displaying a versatility of mind and a resourcefulness short of genius.

Jake Ferguson was about six feet tall, lean, and lanky in his youth, filling out in his later years. Early photos show him with the full face of a man in touch with life, sharp features, aquiline nose, deep set eyes and a turned-down-at-the-corners, unsmiling, "Ferguson" mouth. In one of those photos, he is wearing his Sunday best, a dark vested, pin-striped suit with chain and watch fob, topped off by a white, wide-brimmed fedora, the brim raked at a slant, making him appear slightly cocky. In the picture, he was probably in his handsome fifties. He was plain-spoken and never minced words, but he was also caring and sensitive, traits that surfaced in his children, particularly one named Josie.

Figure 2. Jake wearing the white fedora, young person unknown

I was eight years old when he died. In that short time, the only sharp words he ever spoke to me was an admonishment: "Stop calling your daddy 'Bill.' He's your daddy. Call him 'Daddy.' You hear?"

On another occasion, I was playing in the large yard beneath the pecan trees with my cousins. One of them called me "stupid." Crying, I ran onto the porch where my grandfather was sitting in his white rocker. He pulled me toward him and said, "Look at me." I looked into those deep brown eyes. "What somebody calls you doesn't make you what you are." His hand came down softly on my shoulder. "And don't you ever forget it." I never did. In hindsight, I can see his eyes in my mother's, his voice in hers and his no-nonsense toughness in her character. Always, the toughness.

Being the only grandchildren who lived in nearby New Albany and who visited our grandparents on a regular basis, my brother and I received special treatment. I recall our grandfather riding us around the yard on his mule named George. He showed us how to pick cotton, where the dewberry vines were, and how to pick them without getting scratched. He was in his late seventies in those years and retired from farming, but he

Figure 3. Older Jake with the mule

leased his land and would take us for tractor rides with Hambone, one of his black tenants.

A particular memory comes to mind. One day I was at "the home place," as it was called. I was seven years old; the year was 1949. I recall it because my grandfather died the next year. He asked if I wanted to go "down the hill and watch 'em make sorghum molasses." I had poured molasses onto my biscuits and pancakes but knew nothing else about the slow, sweet syrup.

He took my hand in his and led me down the western slope from the house into a low-lying swampy area, plowed around because it was always wet. I could attempt to tell you what I remembered seeing, but my Aunt Blanche gives a better description:

> The grist mill was not far from our house, and Ruby took me over to watch them. I can see the one from the center feeding the pieces of cane into the press which worked and extracted the juice, made by a blindfolded mule going round and round. The juice was caught in a container, then taken over to a long copper pan ten or twelve feet long with a fire underneath. There were two men with long paddles, stirring the juice as it cooked. This was a three- or four-day procedure and one with many hands helping. The molasses was put in jugs and gallon cans. There was enough for all of us, and Papa sold some in the store in town.

Making sorghum molasses each fall was just one of Jake Ferguson's sources of income. He was an innovative and resourceful entrepreneur, which rings all too familiar.

Though a farmer at heart, in order to provide for his family, Jake believed in looking ahead and diversifying. He cultivated forty acres of cotton and corn with additional pastureland. To utilize the pasture, he bought milk cows and started a dairying enterprise. The cows were mixed breeds—Jersey, Guernsey, Swiss and Holstein. Milking took place in the barn hall. Renting the cropland opened up another opportunity. Jake garnered the position of livestock inspector in Tippah, Union, and Pontotoc counties. Blanche picks up the narrative:

> He was gone all week making those rounds in a two-wheel cart with George hitched to it. With all the skim milk from the dairy, he saw fit to start breeding pure bred Duroc hogs using the skim milk for them with corn thrown in. The pens were beyond the barn with big troughs in each pen. The boar was much taller than I, but that didn't keep us from getting in the pen with him. When the crops were done, Papa had a job waiting for him in town at R. Moore's Dry Goods. This brought him a little more income. Another way he had of making ends meet was spraying and pruning fruit trees. Dr. Sam Eason was at our house often, and Papa cared for Dr. Eason's orchard, which took care of doctor's bills.

Speaking of doctor's bills, Jake was a shade-tree physician with multiple curative specialties. One of his prescriptions called for slippery elm bark, red oak bark, alum, and honey. This concoction was boiled in water, drained off and honey added to obtain a syrup. Blanche notes, "This was our cough medicine. For sore throats, Papa swabbed our throats with diluted iodine. A bad chest cold required a poultice of mustard mixed with lard." Blanche continues, adding this touch:

> The mustard seeds were beaten with lard added, spread on a clean cloth, and put on the chest. It did not need to stay long. Earaches were relieved by making a funnel of light cardboard, placing a cotton of chloroform in the end, inserting into the ear, and blowing. I don't know how affected the blower became, but it gave the patient a pleasant instant relief. Don't ask me how the chloroform was procured.

Jake Ferguson's great pride was the orchard. It was behind the garden and opposite the barn lot. He had planted multiple trees including peach, apple, plum, pear and quince, a hard acid pear-shaped fruit. The produce from these took care of the family's fruit needs, canned or dried. The trees also provided a playground for his children, including a place for climbing, hide-and-go-seek and playhouses.

The orchard area was in a two-acre plot. Jake planted cotton to keep the place clean and to furnish his children with a patch to maintain. Dan plowed it, and Robbie and Blanche chopped it and picked the cotton. As Blanche in her journal observed, "I don't think we made much money, but it was our patch."

School teachers boarded at the house, yet another revenue source. Blanche provided some of the names: Rose Wiseman, Miss Patterson, Miss Anna Swain. The latter married Crack Wells, who became the sheriff of Union County. Jake Ferguson had a way and methodology about him for gaining friends in high places. It wasn't what you knew, but who you knew, a philosophy that would catch on quite well with his children, particularly daughter Josie.

Boarding teachers takes us close to the soul of Jake Ferguson. Aside from all of his entrepreneurial endeavors and exploits, of supreme importance to him was the education of his children. Blanche provides a glimpse of that dedication:

> We lived a mile and a half from school and weather permitting, we walked to and from school. When the weather was bad, Papa took the surrey. There were storm curtain fenders on it and lights on the side to use at night. Papa stopped for all the Marshall Hill school children. Later, when there got to be so many of us, he brought the wagon. The wagon had no seats so one learned to balance early in life. Umbrellas were used. The ruts were deep. I'm sure Papa was afraid axles on the surrey would break. One morning, the rain was pouring and had been pouring all night. The bottom was covered, and the road and the bridge were lost under water. Papa took one of the mules and took us with him one-by-one across the bridge. Mules instinctively know where to put their feet. We had to walk the rest of the way, but we made it across the creek.

Into his late seventies, Jake was in good physical shape. Except for overseeing some of the dairy and sorghum operations, he leased his land and considered himself a gentleman farmer. Daily, he walked the mile-and-a-half to New Albany to sit on the porch of a small ramshackle store just across the bridge at the bottom of Bankhead Street. I remember it was plastered with soft-drink, snuff and tobacco signs and ads. The store is long gone and so is my grandfather. But not my memory of seeing him sitting with his friends on a long bench across the front of the store. On occasional trips running errands with my mother, we'd cross the Tallahatchie Bridge, and she would say, "Wave to your granddaddy." I'd see him sitting on that bench, in the same place, and wave. He'd wave back with a big smile.

Knowing he walked "all the way" from his house to the store every day except Sunday, I was shocked to learn that, on July 5, 1950, he had died. He was 80 years old. His daughter Josie, my mother, was 32. I was eight. It was my first experience with the death of a family member. On reflection, of what I know now, it was also my mother's.

I remember the day of the funeral, my grandmother's trip to our house, how pale and saddened she looked, her glasses pushed back on her forehead, her eyes red. I did not go to the funeral. My brother and I were told to stay home with Lula, our black help. I was upset, so Lula held me and rocked me and sang a song I now know as "Swing Low, Sweet Chariot." Within a short time, the parts of our lives seemed to fall back into place. Except a big part for my mother: her father.

Unquestionably, Jake Ferguson's legacy was the goal of seeing all of his children formally educated in ways he was not. He had succeeded in life because he was the beneficiary of a combination of good genes, frontier know-how and legacies of persistence, hard work, and diversity passed down to him. There are some things, however, not passed along genetically: values and morals. Jake knew this. To ensure their strong transferal to his children, he married a woman in lockstep with his goals and dreams. And his values.

Susie Belle Lamar Ferguson was born March 9, 1873. That year, the American Indian Wars were raging, and President Grant was sworn in for his second term. The stock market crashed triggering the Panic of 1873, and the Long Depression began. P. T. Barnum's circus debuted in New York City, the Women's Christian Temperance Union was created, barbed wire was exhibited at the Illinois State Fair and the Coinage Act placed the nation firmly on the gold standard.

The photographs I have seen of my grandmother portray a beautiful, black-haired woman of medium height, lean with an elegant, svelte demeanor. In those days, I guess people were told by the photographer not to smile, but in her pictures one can see the faint glimmer of one highlighted by her bright eyes.

Figure 4. Belle Lamar Ferguson

Based upon the information available, mostly through Blanche, Belle attended a boarding school at Poplar Springs, a co-educational school located between Pontotoc and Union Counties and graduated from Blue Springs Finishing School for Girls near Tupelo, which was unusual for those times. Blanche adds this touch:

Being a Lamar, Mama had more French genes

running around than Papa could afford or saw any use for and must have hated putting up with a primitive way of life, especially since her home place was much finer and grander … she was used to some of the more refined things even though she may not have been of the manor born.

Belle allowed her children to care for themselves. Jake was in the field, and she had a multitude of household chores that began when she awoke at daybreak and ended when she went to bed, around nine each evening. As a teenager and college student, I often spent nights and days in her home and witnessed, first-hand her routine.

Every morning, after rising and dressing, her first task was stoking the kitchen stove fire and adding kindling. In cold weather, Jake revived the banked coals of the three fireplaces and fired them up. In addition to Belle's daily kitchen cycle of cooking and washing dishes three times a day, she boiled lye in a huge black caldron in the backyard and made soap. She milked cows, gathered eggs, threw grain to the chickens, chopped wood and, if time remained, baked pies, and made ice cream. Her version of ice cream was boiled custard poured into an ice tray and placed in the freezer. (Before she had an electric refrigerator/freezer, she placed the custard-filled trays in an ice box, filled with huge blocks of ice delivered from the icehouse in New Albany.)

Other daily tasks included pumping water from the well, straining whole milk into a churn and churning butter. Later in her childhood, Blanche recalled, "this daily procedure with Mama singing as she churned up and down with the dasher in perfect rhythm," pointing out that in winter it took two days for the milk to turn and reach a clabbered stage.

In season, Belle picked fruit, planted, and gathered vegetables, dried, and canned them. In late summer, the fall garden came in— beets, cabbage, onions, shallots, turnips, and sweet potatoes. Jake had a house for sweet potatoes that required special curing methods. The other vegetables were gathered in the fall. Blanche again:

> A large hole was dug in the garden, one big enough to accommodate a large barrel. The barrel was placed in the hole a little over halfway buried. It was lined with hay and vegetables—turnips, cabbage, Jerusalem artichokes were added. Hay covered these, then piles of hay covered the barrel. Mama could go out and scratch through these for fresh vegetables. This would not keep through the coldest of winter but were good as long as the supply lasted. The turnip green patch and collards lasted through much of winter.

There was always mowing the yard, pulling weeds, feeding ("slopping") the hogs, and watching the hens when they were hatching eggs. I recall one day going to my grandparents' home with my mother and watching my grandmother ring a chicken's neck, blood flying all over her and spraying me, the headless hen running around in circles, flapping her wings, feathers flying everywhere. Finally, after a long time it seemed, the hen toppled over in the dust of the chicken-wire coop. I had nightmares for weeks and wouldn't eat my grandmother's chicken unless it was mixed with rice she prepared with a congealed consistency.

As they grew older, sons Guy and Dan took over the more

strenuous outside chores, and the girls helped their mother. Blanche wrote:

> The usual vegetable, beans, were canned by Mama, May, and Ruby, but some of the picking and string beans were left up to Robbie and me. Cabbage was chopped, layered in salt for kraut, and then the tomatoes were canned, and some made into chili sauce. Beets were pickled as were cucumbers and peaches. Jellicoes were made from wild plums, which Robbie and I plundered through the thickets for. We had a lot of Himalaya blackberries, which Papa had planted among the eroded places. These were excellent for jelly and jam.

If the orchard was Jake's pride, the kitchen was Belle's. Following her death and the celebration of 105 years of life, some of her children compiled a book entitled *Susie Belle's Favorite Recipes*. (See Appendix E)

Figure 5. Belle with family on her 100th birthday sitting on her porch] (Back row standing left to right: Martha Glynn, Josie, Dan, Blanche, Guy and May, Bottom Row seated left to right: Robbie, Belle, Ruby)

In her "free" time, and as she grew older, Susie Belle crocheted foot warmers for all of her grandchildren. Every other year, grandchildren would find a pair of foot warmers under their Christmas tree. I recall my senior year in high school, my mother telling me, "Hang on to these. They'll be the last."

My favorite memories of Grandmama Susie Belle were the nights my brother and I spent with her. We'd crawl onto her quilted bed and have interesting discussions. One night, we asked how old she was. She said 75. That was Methuselah old to us. We'd been studying history in school and began asking questions about what she remembered. She recalled the battleship Maine blowing up in Havana Harbor, Cuba. She said it happened in 1898, and she was 25 years old at the time. "And it got us into a war with Spain," she said to two awestruck grandsons.

Next on our improvised list was the Titanic.

"Why, of course, I remember the sinking of the Titanic. It occurred in 1912. I was thirty-nine years old. Your mother was born six years later."

We wanted to know more specifics. She recalled the number of people lost and something about the survivors. We did not ask about World War I, but she brought it up, told us about Wilson and his fight to keep the U. S. neutral and his League of Nations dream. She was telling us things we had read and forgotten and here she was 75 and rolling them effortlessly off her tongue.

Until.

"Grandmama, what about the Great Depression?"

Her head flinched backward, her eyes narrowed, and a

grim look suddenly gripped her face.

"I don't recall much at all, except it wasn't great."

We pressed for more.

"I don't want to talk about it," was all she would say.

What she could not, or would not say, Blanche, years later, put into words. (See "Depression Days," Appendix C)

Several years later, I drove out to my grandmama's for a visit. At the time, she would have been around 82. I saw her in the side yard between the orchard and the pecan trees constructing something. I got out of the car and walked over to greet her and help her. I do not recall much about the encounter except I was overwhelmed that she was building, of all things, a split-rail fence and for no reason except for aesthetics, separating the orchard from the pecan trees. Perhaps, she had another point to prove.

One thing I do remember, something she said that has served me well in my personal, as well as my professional, life. She was mumbling something about one of my aunts and said to me, "Folks say the grass is greener on the other side. Well, it may be but, Edd, I'm telling you," And she looked me in the eye as though this message was meant for me to remember: "There are just as many weeds over there as there are over here."

Susie Belle Lamar Ferguson died August 23, 1978. She was 105. Her funeral took place in her church, First United Methodist Church in New Albany. Reverend Lavelle Woodrick conducted the funeral service. Her oldest grandson, Bill Ferguson, sang a solo. I was honored to present the eulogy. (See Appendix F)

During their fifty-four years of marriage and following their generational pattern, John Gilliam "Jake" and Susie Belle

Lamar had a large family, nine children (one still-born)—two sons, Guy, and Dan, and six daughters: May, Ruby, Robbie, Blanche, Joan, Martha Glynn. (For bios on the Ferguson siblings see Appendix A.)

Common themes ran through the brood. Despite their humble origins and their father's minimal finances, they all obtained a college education. They were all intelligent and successful in their chosen careers.

Except for May, all married well and successfully. When asked why she didn't marry, May said, as Swift Rogers remembers it: "Papa said for me to marry blue chips, not common stock. But blue chips never came alone."

Not surprisingly, all the Ferguson children were bright, independent, tough, stubborn, competitive, and out-spoken. Their search for knowledge, spirit of adventure and desire to succeed were boundless. They all endured and lived long lives, some longer than others. And each, in many ways, helped shape the woman Joan "Josie" Ferguson would become.

Chapter 3: First Home

Twelve miles away, and the nearest town to Rocky Ford and Etta, was New Albany, Mississippi. The town was established in 1840 on the banks of the Tallahatchie River, "Tallahatchie" a Choctaw Indian name meaning "rock of waters." The river winds 230 miles from its source in Tippah County, Mississippi, and empties into the Yalobusha River forming the Yazoo River. In the Treaty of Pontotoc Creek, the Chickasaw Nation ceded its remaining land in Mississippi to the United States. The treaty specified, however, that each family of the Chickasaw Nation would be granted land, depending upon the size of the family. Additional land was made available with families owning slaves.

On January 25, 1836, President Martin Van Buren granted 640.48 acres of land or section 8, Township7, Range 3 east of the place where the town of New Albany would be located. The recipient was Chickasaw Chief Ia-na-ho-ka-ta. Around 1835, anticipating the sale of public land not granted to the Chickasaws, white settlers began moving into the area. A man named Moses Collins built a gristmill on the Tallahatchie River, which is considered to be the beginning of New Albany. Some new settlers opted for high ground east of the town. Others chose the flat and bottom land west. Small groups met for worship in homes, and sometime, around 1842 and 1843, established the Zion Hill Baptist Church, the forerunner of the First Baptist Church of New Albany. A community began to materialize around the Tallahatchie River. (From *Union County History*)

In 1890, the population of New Albany was 548. By the

time the Fergusons arrived in 1912, it had quadrupled to over 2,000. The town had two newspapers (*The Blakeslee and The Gazette*), two banks (First National and Merchants & Farmers), a Methodist and Baptist church, a school and boarding system, two drug stores and a post office. Several blocks of brick mercantile stores lined its two main streets that extended from the river up its sloping bluffs to the recently constructed mammoth blonde stone courthouse which, in that year, dominated the landscape. During this time, manufacturing was flourishing with a box factory, stave mill, wagon factory and brick kiln. Where the two railroads crossed sat the imposing two-story Rainey Hotel where meals were 50 cents and lodging a dollar. South of the river bridge was the Jockey-yard where men came on Saturdays and sold livestock and country folk parked their wagons to shop.

In 1912, the Tallahatchie, in season, was navigable, another reason Jake Ferguson moved his family to the area. He could put his cotton on steamboats and flatbeds and ship them to the Mighty Mississippi, and ultimately to New Orleans. Other shipping outlets included the two railroads, the east-west Frisco, and the north-south Gulf, Mobile and Ohio (GM&O).

Blanche recalls her father, at certain intervals of farming seasons, taking two or three days off, hitching up the team of mules to the wagon and going to New Albany. The round trip, including stops along the way, took about eight hours.

Jake Ferguson had practical reasons for being attracted to New Albany. The first years of the twentieth century were hard times for Salem and the surrounding communities of Rocky Ford, Etta, Galway, and Mt. Pisgah. Unusually heavy and persistent rain made farming difficult. The bottoms flooded, the farmers could not plant. Few, if any, crops were harvested.

Several families, mostly Lamars, decided to move west to Texas. In 1912, Jake and Susie Belle Ferguson headed east to New Albany.

There may have been another reason for the timing of the move. Guy and May, the oldest of their children, had attended a two-teacher school that was located in the Galway community. It was called Mt. Erin. But the school's grades went only to the eighth. In 1912, May finished eighth grade. There was a good school in New Albany where Guy had been attending, boarding there in the winter months.

The move from Rocky Ford would have taken several days, perhaps weeks. No one knows the exact date or dates. From several accounts, we know it took place in 1912. In her journal, Blanche notes, "Papa was busy gathering," so the transition probably occurred in late fall of that year. The girls—May, Ruby, and Robbie—ages fifteen, thirteen and nine respectively, helped their mother pack and care for Blanche who was four. My mother Josie had not yet appeared on the scene.

The distance from the Ferguson home at Rocky Ford to New Albany was twelve miles. The journey would have taken four to five hours by wagon. Moving all of their household furniture (including Ruby's organ) and belongings probably took several days. The boys, Guy and Dan, ages seventeen and eleven respectively, assisted. Both were mature, strong, and able-bodied. Neighbors, no doubt, chipped in.

The final moving day arrived and the entire family—four adolescents, a nine and a four-year-old—climbed aboard the wagon and found places to sit among the last articles loaded. The weather was cool and crisp. Jake Ferguson slapped the reins across the backs of their team of mules, and the wagon lurched eastward toward Etta. Just outside of Etta, the wagon entered Highway 30, a graveled road connecting Oxford and New Albany. They crossed the Little Tallahatchie River and its wide valley, fields of bare cotton stalks gliding by stretching to the wooded horizon. They passed through the village of Enterprise, then dipped into Locke's Creek Valley and crossed Locke's Creek. Past Locke's Creek, the road angled upward and through the hamlet of Poolville, also known as Bugscuffle.

An explanation for the name is in order. It seems the principal of the one room school there, a man named Blizzard, is responsible for the name. Arriving early mornings to fire up the potbelly stove, he said, "The bugs would scuffle across the floor." Bugscuffle. It stuck. He later became the county school superintendent. He and his wife moved to New Albany and resided on Cleveland Street across from Bill and Joan Morris. Their son, Devan, would become my mom's last companion and love on this earth.

Past Poolville, the road sloped downward and leveled out into another valley. The name of the small river and bottom have baffled local historians. The land was some of the most fertile in the state, its crop production prodigious. Why anyone would name a pastoral setting Hell Creek Bottom defied logic. But that was the name and one, I am sure, that sparked questions aboard the rambling wagon on that day.

The family's destination was a house Jake had purchased on the eastern slope of Marshall Hill, named for a prominent family who first inhabited the elevated rise of land overlooking New Albany. The house was still occupied, but Jake had found temporary lodging nearby, a two-story saltbox. (From Blanche's essay "Growing up on Marshall Hill," see Appendix B)

While living in that temporary house on Marshall Hill, Blanche records a memorable event:

> One night, the sky lighted up so much it waked us. The whole town was on fire. We all piled out of bed, put on our clothes, and walked to town. Paul J. Rainey was a millionaire from up east. He had built a fine lodge and had a huge plantation at Cotton Plant, Mississippi, just in Tippah County. Then he built a big hotel, which had a fine arcade attached with a number of stores inside. This was on fire. It was the finest building New Albany ever had. It had a large brick patio-type on the front with tables all along with white coated drakes jumping all over the place. It had class. There it goes. There were all kinds of rumors of arson. It closed the book on a glorious past where balls were held, and people came from far and near to the dances.

That same year, Jake bought "the Louis place" that was farther west over Marshall Hill. Josie would not enter the world for another four years, but this would be the house where she would grow up, an anchor for many years to come. Blanche describes Josie's first home:

> Our new house was larger. It was a Victorian style cottage and had a portico with all the gingerbread around it. The front door had a half glass, and the house was painted. That year, the bed came out of the parlor and replaced the black leather mission style davenport. This was an early version of a hide-a-bed. It was still the guest's room, and I assure you guests didn't stay

long after sleeping on it. The wallpaper was tan in a color called oatmeal, which was a name very apropos. The rug was a cheap—maybe wool—with a geometric design in it. I'm quite sure there were curtains and, of course, the organ which Ruby could play. There was a fireplace with Grandma or Grandpa Ferguson's portraits over the mantle. Having a painted house was a bit more prestigious than the nonpainted and a brick walk out to the road. On each side of the porch were two rose bushes, cream-colored roses, and Mama knew their names.

The place had been an old established home. The garden was filled with perennial plants including sage, shallots, Jerusalem artichokes and berries in the back area. There were fruit trees in the garden, but, living out his dream, Jake transplanted them in a large area designated for his orchard. Blanche's description continues:

> The outbuildings were a very important thing in our lives. A few steps behind the house was the smokehouse. It had a flue, many shelves for dried and canned fruits, and the floor was three or four inches deep in grease-soaked dirt, sawdust or whatever. The chicken/hen house was closer to the barn behind the buggy shed. There was a tin house with a window and a flue, which possibly was a servants' house at one time. The driveway was between the buggy shed and this metal house. A big gate into the barn lot was there also. In the buggy shed was the surrey and the wagon. The barn was the jewel of them all. It had a big shed

outside going almost the length of it. At one end was the "tack" room for it held the saddle, bridles and all the harnesses needed for the surrey and the wagon. Under one end of the covered part was the riding cultivator where plows were kept in the tack room also. Gates opened into the barn hall. On one side was the corncrib and on the same side were the milking stalls, two of them with stalls for the cows, open air but covered. On the other side of the hall where the enclosed stall for the horses. The only source of light was the open hall. Calves were kept in a stall by the milking stalls.

By the corncrib was the ladder. This was our approach to the hayloft. At the top of the ladder was the big opening into the loft, which we became very adept at scooting in and out. The big opening had to be large enough to pitch the hay through for the livestock. The hayloft was a multi-purpose place. Circuses were performed there, and we played hide and seek, hiding from the enemy and exploring it by tunneling through the hay.

Those who knew Josie would agree. This was the perfect place for her debut.

Chapter 4: Early School Years

In 1918, six years after Jake moved his family from Rocky Ford to New Albany, on March 9—her mother's birthday—Joan "Josie" Ferguson was born.

Headlines in the New York Times read: GERMAN RAIDS OVER LONDON KILL 11. Earlier that year, President Woodrow Wilson had delivered his Fourteen Points speech, and Congress had established time zones and Daylight Savings Time. In 1918, the U. S. Post Office began regular airmail service between New York City, Philadelphia and Washington, D.C., and on November 11, World War I ended.

This was the epochal, effervescent, changing world Josie entered.

She was Jake and Susie Belle's seventh child. Her oldest brother, Guy, was out of college and had his first job. Her two oldest sisters, May and Ruby were in college. Two months later, Dan would graduate from high school and leave for college. At home were Robbie, age 15, and Blanche, 10. These two sisters became Josie's principle caretakers. In three years, Robbie would be gone, off to college, and Blanche would have a three-year-old on her hands. Two years after my mother's birth, another sister, Martha Glynn, was born, adding another responsibility for Blanche. Little wonder that in years later she embarked on an elementary education career.

In March of 1918, New Albany, Mississippi was continuing to grow. Jill Smith, Director of the Union County Historical Society and Museum, offered these tidbits:

Roads had been improved; concrete sidewalks laid. In

1912, a sewage system had been added. Cleveland Street Elementary School had been built in 1913, and Home Demonstration began in 1916. Mrs. H. B. Wiseman was the first home demonstration agent, and one of the early workers was Coy Hines, later to become Mrs. John Stennis. Scott Parks' Cash Store was advertising in *The Gazette* for all ladies to visit the Millinery Dept. and to make the store's restroom their "headquarters" while shopping in town. Apparently, this was the public restroom. Men's suits costs $11.75 at J.G. Houston and Co. and a "run-about" Ford car sold for $390. A sedan cost $740. The Dreamland Theater was in business. The feature for March 30, 1917 was The Iron Claw starring Pearl White, a native of Mississippi. The Rainey Hotel was destroyed by fire in 1915 taking several businesses with it and these were all located on Cotton Street, which later became Bankhead Street.

World War I came to New Albany when 5 young men volunteered on April 12, 1917. Liberty Bond drives began with a flag raising ceremony on May 10. And on June 6 a parade was held by men of registerable age. That day, 1,050 young men registered, and the first 10 left for Camp Pike, Arkansas. The Red Cross was organized August 1, 1917, and by Christmas had 900 members who worked tirelessly, helping war families, and knitting many socks and rolling bandages. Two New Albany boys lost their lives in this war, Guy Potter and Curtis Henry.

Despite the progress that had come to New Albany, much of it had not "crossed the Tallahatchie bridge." Josie's early years were spent in a pioneer, primitive, rural, farm world. The home on Marshall Hill, though only a mile from New Albany, had no electricity and no indoor plumbing. Looking back, some might call that life then was one of hardship. But the Fergusons did not know that word. The Great Depression had not yet hit. The economy was upward bound. Jake Ferguson was a hardworking, successful farmer. The luxury of that time was "making ends meet."

When she was old enough to walk, with Blanche as her caretaker, Josie was probably given something to carry, even if it was a stick of wood. She often picked up pecans or ripened fruit that had fallen to the ground. I imagine her walking behind her mother to the chicken coop, being given grains of corn to toss, and then hiding in her mom's skirts when the chickens came after it. Surely, she accompanied someone to the hen house for egg collecting.

As she grew older, I can see my grandmother, or Blanche, showing young Josie how to churn butter. When vegetables were harvested, these two women taught Josie how to shell peas, shuck corn and snap beans. Forbidden to go near the well, Josie would go around and beyond it to the dewberry patch. She went once, and, as word came down, she never went again. Not because of the stickers. She saw a snake that was summarily decapitated with a hoe by her mother.

In the fall of 1925, Josie entered the first grade. Based upon the history available, she attended the New Albany Elementary School in a facility that was constructed in 1901, the first building in New Albany specifically built for the purpose of education. According to the history in the city's sesquicentennial souvenir book, the school had two stories, with a full basement (including a steam boiler room and toilets), 18 classrooms, offices and a large auditorium which served as a study hall. The facility also sported a tower housing its bell.

In 1913, the Cleveland Street Elementary School was built to accommodate students who lived on the north side of town from grade one to grade four. Because of an increase in enrollment, an addition to that building in 1926 added the fifth and sixth grades.

Bayard Coulter, who served as superintendent from 1920 to 1928, envisioned a new high school building and a new elementary school on the south side of town. In 1926, Central Elementary School was constructed on the grounds of the old high school building. Josie's first grade class, therefore, was the last first grade class to use the 1901 building before it was demolished. She entered second grade in the new facility for the elementary and high schools. That year, 1926, Miss Mattie Pennebaker became the elementary principal and W. P. Daniel, the superintendent. The new brick structure on Apple Street had wings for the elementary and high school, both connected by a long hall and an auditorium.

Information on Josie's elementary years is scarce. Because of the discipline that shaped the lives of all the Ferguson children, homework came before chores, chores before play. Josie was a good student and made excellent grades. Early to bed and rising early were part of the routine. Going to bed early, according to her mother, meant eight o'clock. There was no television then and only one radio in the house. More people had cars then and it is likely that Josie, instead of riding in a wagon, was taken to school in the family's only car or carpooled with others on Marshall Hill.

During the depression years, Josie was attending school in

New Albany. She and Martha Glynn rode to school in her father's farm wagon with facing benches in the bed. The roads were dirt, and in the winter four mules had to pull the wagon. Josie took her lunch to school in a molasses bucket. Huge, buttered biscuits with jelly were a mainstay along with some ham and sausage, plus a piece of cake or teacake. Before she left home early in the morning, often before sunrise, breakfast consisted of pot-boiled coffee, ham, sausage or fatback, eggs, blackberry jelly or jam, and great big white, two-story biscuits.

During those times, powerful educational forces were at work and have continued to influence school excellence in the "Fair and Friendly City." Backing up a couple of decades, in 1907 New Albany High School received accreditation from the Association of Colleges and Secondary Schools, having the honor of being the third school in the state to achieve this status. Prior to W. P. Daniel's tenure, Bayard L. Coulter (1920-1928) established the first science lab in north Mississippi. Until then, the closest one was in Meridian. That science lab would have an immeasurable influence on Josie's life. Again, from the sesquicentennial archives:

> In 1921, Mr. Coulter secured Miss Marjorie Scott, a 19-year-old native of Lucedale, to implement the project. Her instructions were to procure all necessary equipment for a science lab as well as for a wireless transmitting and receiving station. Miss Scott set up the lab and, until her marriage to J. G. Houston in 1923, taught high school Science, including physics.

Marjorie Houston would become my mother's spiritual mentor and, along with others, was responsible for her progressive views on civil rights and theology. Josie was also significantly influenced by another teacher.

In 1932, The Depression was ending, and Mary Davidson began a ten-year stint as high school math teacher. Her principal was J. E. Long. He later became the pastor of the Methodist Church in New Albany and years later, my District Superintendent in the North Mississippi United Methodist Conference. Another teacher and future Methodist pastor of the Methodist Church was Audie Bishop. Mary Davidson would marry Clyde Hall. Because classrooms were scarce, Hazel Smallwood, who was teaching English and Latin, taught with Mary in the dressing rooms, which flanked the stage of the auditorium.

The 1933 New Albany High School Yearbook provides more information on "Josie" Ferguson and New Albany High School. It was the first high school yearbook of many to be published over subsequent years. W. P. Daniel was the Superintendent and W. G. Rutledge the Principal. Faculty names included G. D. Hightower, coach; M. L. Burkes, science; Miss Corrie Stewart, music; Miss Sara Coker, music; Mrs. Lanier Nisbet, Latin; Mrs. Frank Caldwell, 7th Grade; Mrs. Jim Hudspeth, math; Mrs. Bill Smallwood, English; Mrs. Katie May Ivey, Commercial Department; Mrs. Billy Rogers, English; Miss Marion Bingham, history; Mrs. Henry King, expression; Miss Mary Davidson, math and Miss Mary Joan Finger, Librarian.

In 1933, Josie was in the ninth grade. Friends in her class included Roscoe Bryson, Ruth Blizzard, Bill Harwell, Manning Hudson, Dan Pitner, Herbert Rogers Jr., Rebecca Poe, and Odie Speck. The freshman class motto was, "Seize the Opportunity," one that could not have defined my mother and her future more appropriately.

Josie's name was listed on the girls' basketball team roster. She was easy to pick out in the group photograph. No information about the team and her performance was available. More likely than not, the basketball schedule included the following schools: Center, Poolville, Pinedale (where she would later teach), Myrtle, Ingomar and Wheeler.

Figure 6. Class with Josie on back row ... "circled"

Josie was tall. In most group pictures, from high school through her class reunions, Joan Ferguson is always on the back row, flashing that trademark challenging smirk.

In the 1933 basketball team photo, she is in the center, kneeling, hands on her knees, her hair style the same that would follow her to the end of her life.

Figure 8. The Basketball Team ... Josie circled

Reflecting upon her life, upon her aggressiveness and persistence, upon that challenging and confrontational spirit, there is little doubt that Josie, regardless the position she played, was one helluva basketball player. But I think, with a touch of irony, that she relished being, and playing, center.

The senior class that year of 1933 had Mrs. W. C. Smallwood as its sponsor; Mary Hudson, President; Dick Marchbanks, Vice-President and Sam McCurry, Secretary Treasury. Members of that graduating class included Malcolm Hall, Everette Hawthorne, Baxter Knox, Jr., William Neely, David Purnell, Boyce Snipes, Pearl Cruse (Deaton), Deloris Fuller, Ruth McAllister, and Inez Nabors.

I did not pick these names at random. All of these senior class members became Josie's good friends and also served the community of New Albany well.

Some members of the Junior Class of 1933 also, at some point, became close friends and confidants of my mother:

Devan Blizzard, Lee Rogers, Edgar Stephens, and Mabel Poyner (Bryson). Devan "Bill" Blizzard would reenter my mother's life in a powerful and meaningful way, but that story must wait. Lee Rogers would own Rogers Rexall Drug Store next to my mother and father's jewelry store.

In the 8th grade below her, Josie forged lasting friendships with Tom Hunt Cole, Norma Craig, Elizabeth, and Travis Ferguson (no relation), Thomas Hawthorne, Malcolm Jackson, Louise Kitchens, Tom Poe, Nat Rogers, William Shannon, Edith Speck and Hugh Marion Stephens.

Years later, in 1959 and 1996, when the class of '36 needed someone to organize their class reunions, it turned to Josie, ever the motivator and driving spirit ("Seize the Opportunity"). Her attention to detail and thoroughness are revealed in a 1996 letter to class members. (See Appendix D)

GIRLS' GLEE CLUB

Elizabeth Hall — President
Ruth Agner — Vice-President
Juadine Middleton — Secretary-Treasurer
Miss Nell Wynn — Director

Edith Mitchell
Joan Ferguson
Helen Waldrop
Ernestine Wells
Miss Nell Wynn
Kathryn Wamble
Lorraine Smith
Dorothy Wilkins
Juadine Middleton
Marguerite Smith
Dorothy Cox
Warrene Smith
Ruth Moore
Helen Eudy

Sue Jones
Elizabeth Hall
Mildred Thrailkill
Madie Moore Worthington
Jeffie Windham
Leuneil Trotter
Dorothy Ann Jinkins
Katherine Lamb
Helen Frances Clay
Mary Elizabeth Alexander
Ruth Agner
Marvin Purnell
Maureen Turner

Figure 10. Delta State Teachers College Glee Club

Chapter 5: College Days and First Job

In the spring of 1936, Josie graduated from New Albany High School. That summer, she spent helping at home and preparing for her matriculation at Delta State Teachers College in Cleveland, Mississippi, heart of the Mississippi Delta. Though the details are unknown, she had received notice of a scholarship. Although she excelled in basketball, the award was not an athletic scholarship. Women's basketball had not come to Delta State in 1936. She had, however, been an honor roll student. Regardless the source of the funds, Papa Jake was proud to have another daughter in college. Her sisters before her May, Ruby, Robbie, and Blanche had had academic scholarships.

Little is known of Josie's tenure at Delta State. Her picture appears in *The Broom,* the school yearbook. She was in the Glee Club, possibly a connection with a scholarship. Jake pulled out all the stops for his children's educations. Josie enrolled in liberal arts with a goal of getting a degree in elementary education. She stayed for one year.

The reason, or reasons, Josie did not return to Delta State are unknown. Perhaps it was The Delta and its foreign, free-wheeling culture. Or, for that same reason, her father determined she needed to go elsewhere. Her scholarship might have been for only one year. Did she fall in love, and the man broke off the relationship? Or did she break it off? Possibly, Jake got a better deal, a better scholarship. Digging deeper, could it have had to do with something far more intriguing?

Knowing my mother's penchant for nonconventional dress, I found this item in the college's 1940 Green Book, which contained the campus rules and regulations:

> Young women students are expected to appear on the campus in conventional dress. The wearing of bloomers, trousers, and shorts is confined to the athletic field and gymnasium. Young women who appear off the campus, in the library, academic hall, dining hall, or reception halls are expected to appear in conventional dress.

Regardless of the reason, not only did Josie not return to Delta State in the spring of 1937; she did not go to college anywhere. Her whereabouts in the school year 1937-38 are a mystery. (Blue Mountain College Records showed she attended in 1966 for a semester and audited a course in home decorating and interior design.) Presumably, for financial reasons, she came home and worked for a year. If so, no one living knows where she worked. Whatever she did during that year, it did not stop her from returning to college.

In the fall of 1939, as the school's records indicate, Josie enrolled at Hinds Junior College as a sophomore. The school was located just outside of Jackson, the Mississippi state capital. At that time, the college was a four-to-five-hour drive by car or bus from New Albany. But Josie was in luck. In 1935, The Gulf, Mobile and Northern Railroad had begun providing service between Jackson, Tennessee, Jackson, Mississippi, and New Orleans. The train, called *The Rebel*, had dining and sleeper coaches and an observation car. In short, Josie went to college in high style.

Except for occasional trips to Memphis and her year at Delta State, it's a good guess riding *The Rebel* was Josie's first time to travel far from home and the beginning of a legacy of travel. She was going to parts of the world she had never seen.

To get to New Albany, *The Rebel* departed Jackson, Tennessee, and made stops at places Josie knew—Ripley, Blue Mountain and Cotton Plant. Past New Albany, there were stops at Ecru, Pontotoc, Mantee, Louisville, Philadelphia, Sebastopol (Russian/Ukranian influence?), Goshen Springs and, eventually, Jackson, Mississippi. She would have boarded The Rebel in New Albany at the old depot (no longer standing), across the street from the imposing Rainey Hotel.

As a young boy, I recall *The Rebel* stopping in the middle of downtown New Albany, the dining car in full view, travelers eating on white tablecloths, a vase of flowers between them, a blur of luxury from which I, at the time, felt barred. I dreamed of someday riding a train and eating in a dining car. I cannot imagine how it must have felt for young Josie.

According to the schedule, *The Rebel* departed New Albany at 5:50 a.m. and arrived in Jackson at 10:30 p.m., a duration of almost 16 hours. (The alternate scheduled boarding was at 11:00 p.m., arriving in Jackson at 6:15 a.m.) The rate was two cents per mile. From New Albany to Jackson was 302 miles for a grand total of $6.04. Without question, if funds were available, something Fergusons had a knack at achieving, on weekends Josie rode *The Rebel* from Jackson to New Orleans and experienced her first international port of call.

In 1937, the effects of the Great Depression were still being felt. But the tempo of life was picking up. Franklin Delano Roosevelt was running for president against Kansas governor Alf Landon. In Mississippi, Martin S. Conner was the governor. He was term-limited and unable to run again, and Hugh White was inaugurated as Mississippi's 45th governor.

The new Hinds County Courthouse had been built in 1930 and was a showpiece of Art Deco. Eudora Welty published her first short story, "Death of a Traveling Salesman," and *Faulkner's Absalom, Absalom* was published. Closer to home, on April 5 a tornado devastated Tupelo, Mississippi.

Josie kept up with the fashion styles, but more often than not, the styles had to keep up with her. In the 30's and the years she went to college, fashion was highly influenced by stars of the silver screen. Men dressed up, sporting fedoras and double-breasted overcoats. Women wore dresses and kept their hair close to their head. Fur was in, and so were floral patterns. Makeup was chic, and shoulder pads were important.

Hats were still popular for women though gradually becoming less popular, except for Josie. What hats did for her and what she did for hats are legendary. In 1936 particularly, women enjoyed wearing a plum or dark green wool tailored dress with long, tight sleeves and slightly bloused bodice, the dress gently flaring at mid-calf with side pleats and often worn with a leather belt.

Gather these fashion images and pictures of Josie—good-looking with a winsome personality, a touch of flare and sashay—entering the lobby of the Edwards Hotel or The Heidelberg or Le Fleurs restaurant.

Figure 11 The King Edward Hotel

Figure 12 Hotel Heidelberg

It is doubtful she went to the Wagon Wheel nightclub on Capitol Street, but it was there at the time, along with other exciting venues in the capitol city for this farm girl come to town and be noticed.

And she *was* noticed.

My first introduction to this story occurred when I was in the store one afternoon sweeping. I was up front behind one of the glassed-in counters that displayed silverware. This man in a suit came swaggering through the front door with a flair, and my mother let out a whoop. The man hugged her and shook my hand, then my father's, though my father did not seem to be that happy to see the man and gave him a grim look. Then, he swung that look, like a turret on a battleship, onto mother.

Later, much later, the story, with details, came down to me. When Josie was attending Hinds Junior College, she was shopping in a local jewelry store. Imagine that. A robbery occurred in the store, and she was a witness. Many months after the event, a prominent attorney in Jackson contacted Josie and wanted her to testify in the case. My mother informed this well-known attorney that she could not testify because she and my father were getting married. The attorney would not accept "No" for an answer and offered to put them up at the hip, Art Deco hotel, The Heidelberg. Mom and Dad loved to dance, and the Victory Room rooftop ballroom was the in place where people danced the night away. Jokingly, Mom used to say that the attorney paid for her trousseau.

The man lingered a while in the store that day, shaking hands with the sales ladies and handing out cards. He gave me a card and said, "Someday you'll be able to vote." I must confess. When I was voting age, and he ran for governor on his third try, I did not vote for Ross Barnett.

Ross Barnett was not the only state politician who admired Josie. Another was from Webster County. He was born August 3, 1901. While in law school, he won a seat in the Mississippi House of Representatives and held that office from 1928 until 1932. After serving as a prosecutor and state judge, he won a special election to fill the Senate vacancy that occurred following the death of Theodore G. Bilbo, won re-election to a full term in 1952 and remained in the Senate until 1988 when he refused to seek another full term. The politician was John C. Stennis.

I am unsure of the connection between Josie and John Stennis, when and where it occurred. One possibility was his marriage to Coy Hines. Both were from Webster County. Sometime after 1916, she taught in the Home Demonstration Department at New Albany High School. Josie was not even born then, arriving on the scene two years later. She entered high school in the 9th grade in 1930. By that time, Coy would have returned to Webster County where she and John Stennis were wed on Christmas Eve in 1929.

I have considered another theory. Stennis might have met my mother when she was at Hinds College and in Jackson when he was a state representative. But that theory was quickly shot down. Stennis left the state House of Representatives in 1932 and became a prosecuting attorney, a position he held until 1937. In the small world of Mississippi in 1937, he could have been the prosecuting attorney in the criminal trial where my mother was a witness and Ross Barnett the defense attorney. Closer to home, Stennis' wife was the sister of Union County Board of Supervisor Buster Hines' wife. In that small world of Mississippi, there is always the possibility that word simply got around that, arguably, Joan Ferguson was one of the best-looking women in Mississippi.

Regardless how they met, John C. Stennis was fond of my mother. I am not suggesting anything inappropriate, but he was an admirer and a loyal devotee. My brother and I both have stories to underscore that fact.

My brother David recounts times he had business in Washington, and all he had to do was call Senator Stennis' office and give his name. "He would always take my call and personally talk with me and always asked about Mom and told me to give her his regards."

David told of a NATO sponsored conference on leadership at Oxford University that was full and not accepting more applicants. David was in England opening an office and wanted to go to the conference. Sitting in the office of the lady who was the administrator organizing the conference in London, he asked her if he could just stand at the back of the room. She told him, "NO WAY!"

David persisted. She asked if he knew anyone in the U. S. He told her John Stennis. She seemed not to believe him and proceeded to call Senator Stennis' office. The next thing he knew, she was handing the phone to David. Stennis was on the line asking him about his mother, to be sure and say hello to her for him and give her his regards. He told David to hand the phone back to the lady. In short, she gave my brother a seat on the front row and a seat at the luncheon table with the speakers and asked he if needed transportation or rooms while in London.

When I heard this story, I thought it was *deja vu* because a similar incident had happened to me. The time was June 1967. More specifically, June 13. I was serving an internship at Reston Redeemer Methodist Church in Reston, Virginia, just outside of Washington, D. C. Al Coppedge, a good friend, and college classmate from the University of Edinburgh where we had completed a year of study, was working in the office of a congressman from his Atlanta, Georgia district. I believe the congressman's name was Blackburn, but his name is immaterial to the story.

Al asked if I wanted to join him at the Capital to sit in on the beginning of the Dodd hearings. Senator Thomas J. Dodd was under scrutiny by the Senate Ethics Committee for ethical violations and improprieties. It is interesting to note that the U. S. Senate was breaking new ground with the inquiry because there were no ethic laws at the time. John Stennis was the chairman of the Ethics Committee. Al and I met on the steps of the Capitol. He ushered me to the door where we could enter the balcony and witness the hearings for that day. He told the doorman he was Representative Blackburn's intern for the summer and showed the man his credentials. We were told only reserved seats remained; therefore, we were denied entrance.

I had an idea. My mother knew Senator John Stennis and had told me if ever I needed a friend in Washington to contact him and tell him Joan Ferguson was my mother.

I had been following Al around and now asked him to follow me. We went to the Senate chamber where the Dodd debates were about to start. On the back of a Capitol brochure, I scribbled a note, cluing Al in on what I was doing. He stood there tapping his toe with an "Oh, sure" look on his face. I handed the note to the doorman and asked him to hand it to Senator Stennis. I could see Stennis through the door near the lectern. I watched the doorman hand the note to Senator Stennis, whose face brightened as he read it. He immediately came to the door, shook hands with Al and me. His first words were, "How's your mother?"

He said he had little time because he was chair of the proceedings that were about to begin. I explained why we were there and that we had been denied entry to the gallery. He pulled a card from his pocket, wrote something on the back and said, "Hand this to the gallery doorman." As we parted, he said, "Give your mother my regards. She's a fine lady." He and I shook hands again.

Al and I returned to the balcony doorman. I handed him the card. We were immediately ushered to front row seats. We spent the entire day in total awe observing Bobby and Ted Kennedy, Irv Dirkson, Eugene McCarthy, Russell B. Long, James O. Eastland, J. W. Fulbright, Margaret Chase Smith, Sam Ervin, Strom Thurmond, Jacob Javits, Robert Byrd, Edmund Muskie, George McGovern, Walter Mondale, and the list goes on. Vice-President Herbert Humphrey was manning the gavel and banged it when the debate turned rancorous, as it often did.

Stennis was gallant and magnanimous in keeping the focus on track and not allowing divergent discussions. Watching him, I kept wondering how my mother knew him. Or was it the other way around. I am still wondering.

I felt ten feet tall and in total awe that day watching history take place on the floor of the United States Senate, our great democracy percolating before my very eyes, seeing the great men now gone and hearing their great voices now stilled. Al Coppedge was taking it all in, too. At the end of the day as we left, he knew I had a friend in a high place and that it was my mother's friend. Two years later, on a trip out west, he stopped in New Albany for a visit. It was not so much to see me as to meet the woman responsible for what happened on June 13, 1967. He was not disappointed. Before getting into his car, as he was leaving the next morning, he looked at me and said, "Now, I know why."

Later, back in New Albany, I shared the Washington story with my mother. She smiled. "He's a dear man." That was all she said, all she needed to say.

While attending Hinds Junior College working towards an elementary teacher's degree, two other important events occurred in Josie's life. She met Jackie Marchant and M. J. (Margaret Joyce) Black, who would become two of her lifelong closest friends. According to my mother, the three met at Hinds. Jackie and M. J. were married, Jackie to a Dutch businessman who spoke with a thick accident and M. J. to William "Bill" Black who was stationed at a near-by air force base.

The details of how they met are unknown, but Josie attracted people, especially those of quality and class. That the three women were clones of each other, guaranteed a "musketeer" union. Over the years, their lives intersected, and often when they did, I was present and privileged to be witness to those convivial times and special relationships.

Almost 20 years later, as a student at Millsaps College, I frequented some of the same places my mom had graced—The Coach and Six in The Heidelberg, The Victory Room, dances at the King Edward (renamed in 1954 by new owners), romantic encounters at LeFleurs. I thought of her, where she might have sat, whom she might have met, all the time envisioning her as pretty, stylishly dressed, a touch of flamboyance.

She attended Hinds Junior College for one year. She did

not attend college for four years, nor did she obtain a degree. In those days, options for a teacher's certificate included a two-year and a four-year curriculum. The two-year curriculum authorized the person for a five-year elementary teaching certificate. The four-year program provided a lifetime certificate (elementary or high school).

Josie opted for the two-year curriculum and came home to teach. An elementary position was available at the Pinedale County School, near her parents' old home place at Etta. Having taught there ten years before, Blanche may have been a factor in her getting the job. Papa Jake also had connections. In the fall of 1940, Josie began teaching in a county school. Based upon letters I discovered postdated from Etta, she boarded in the area and came home on the weekends.

On one weekend trip home, her future took off.

Chapter 6: The Watchmaker

Joan Ferguson had numerous suitors. They came from far and near. Some were men her age, just starting out, with good jobs and promising futures. Some were already successful, professional men, prestigious and in high places. Then, along came a man with lower financial and social status. But he had a charm and an integrity that eclipsed all others.

William Edward "Bill" Morris was born July 13, 1904, in Gault, Missouri, a small town in Grundy County in the northern part of that state. He was the youngest son in a family of two older brothers and three sisters. Soon after his birth, his father, Harry Morris, a local politician, moved the family of eight to nearby Trenton, the county seat. For thirty years, his father served as deputy county clerk and for forty years, secretary of the Trenton School Board, the two positions overlapping.

My father attended Trenton Elementary School and graduated from Trenton High School with honor roll grades. During the Great Depression, he became a watch repair apprentice to William Pennell who had an established watch repair and jewelry business in Trenton. Mr. Pennell eventually moved to Santa Cruz, California, where he made a fortune in the jewelry business. My dad must have filed that success story back, along with a piece of advice from his mentor: "Bill, during bad times, four professions survive: clergy, bootleggers, undertakers and watch repairmen. Regardless how destitute they are, folks' lives depend upon time."

At some point around 1930, Bill Morris, unaware of her

drug and alcohol history, married a lady named Meredith. Her maiden name is unknown to me. Bill had to place Meredith in a sanitarium, and he obtained a divorce. During the time in that marriage, he moved to Jackson, Tennessee, and opened a watch repair and jewelry store. The business lasted seven years and then went bankrupt, in part due to issues surrounding his marriage. He owed significant debt to major watch, jewelry, and China companies. Ball, DeHaviland and Bulova are names that come to mind. I would learn later that, despite his bankruptcy filing, he eventually, little by little, repaid every debt in full and beyond the legal percentage requirements of bankruptcy.

In 1939—broke, debt-ridden, divorced, his life at its lowest point—Bill Morris headed south to see his brother Byron who owned a watch repair and jewelry store in Corinth, Mississippi. Byron told him of a watch repair opportunity in a thriving community fifty miles away. The fact New Albany, Mississippi was a railroad hub loomed large in the decision. Railroad men needed their watches in sync and running on time. "It's all about timing," Dad recalled his brother telling him.

From Corinth, in a model T Ford, Bill Morris drove to New Albany with only five dollars in his billfold, his watch repair equipment and the watch bench from Mr. Pennell's store that he had lugged around with him. He rented a room for a dollar a night with meals at a large boarding house on Bankhead Street, which, at that time, stood on the property now occupied by the Bank of New Albany. Next door, looking east, was the post office, now the Main Street offices.

Figure 13. Bill Morris taken about the time he came to New Albany

His first day in New Albany, Bill Morris would have descended the steps of the boarding house. He probably crossed the street and headed west down Bankhead passing Bell's Blue Star grocery, a large brick house (where a chiropractor had hung a shingle), City Hall and the corner drugstore. At the drugstore, he would have crossed the GM&O tracks, passed the Bank of New Albany, Lowrey's Dry Goods,

Rogers' Rexall Drug Store, an unknown retail store (later to become Morris Jewelry Store) and West's Grocery, stopping at the next building: Gray's Drugstore.

That name had been provided to him by his brother, Byron, whose store in Corinth was near a Borroum's Drug Store, and the proprietor had given him the name of Gray's. The tip paid off. Mr. Gray, the owner, told Bill he could set up his repair bench at the front of the store in the window where passersby could see him. A sign, WATCH REPAIR SERVICE, was placed in the window. As part of the arrangement, Bill agreed to pay Mr. Gray a percentage of his gross earnings.

In a matter of days, Bill Morris was repairing watches. The railway engineers and switchmen had heard about him and began stopping by to check their large fob watches. Word spread and a steady stream of customers made its way to Gray's Drug Store to get their watches fixed. Others in the town and county had learned he could fix more than watches.

Not to be outdone by older sister Blanche, who had taken up cello lessons, Josie Ferguson decided she would learn to play the violin. How my mother came by a violin in those days is still a mystery. Blanche played a cello and had music connections, which may have been a factor in Josie's decision.

My mother discovered one of the small screws in her violin case was loose. She had tried to tighten it with a fingernail, a fingernail file and even a razor blade, as she told the story. Nothing worked. Then she heard there was a watchmaker in town who had tiny screwdrivers.

What happened that day when she walked through the door at Gray's Drug Store and saw my father, and he saw her, has never been difficult for either of them to put into words.

Josie: "I stopped in my tracks. I was expecting some old

man wearing glasses with gray hair and bushy eyebrows, not somebody that looked like Clark Gable."

Bill: "I was working on a watch, and when I looked up, I almost dropped it. Standing before me was the most beautiful woman with knockout legs I'd ever seen."

The conversation between them that day is long gone. Bill Morris fixed her violin case. Within a week, she was back. A screw had fallen from the temple of her glasses. The next week, it was her watch. "It just keeps the wrong time, Bill." He recalled she used his first name. He pulled out the stem, aligned the shorthand with the long hand, popped the stem back in and wound it a few times. "I think it's fine, Joan. You must've somehow misaligned the hands." He handed it back to her with a smile, and then asked her for a date.

She recalled they went to The Ritz movie theater where Blanche worked in the ticket booth. (The Ritz was further down Bankhead toward the river, below The WhiteWay Cafe and next to Sherman's Dry Goods.) It was a Friday night. He asked Josie for dinner the next night. They ate in the rebuilt ornate Rainey Hotel dining room.

One of the clerks in Gray's said Josie became a regular at the soda fountain and "Mr. Bill was buying her Cokes." My father maintained a counter slush fund for her drinks in case he was busy and couldn't personally pay.

According to one substantiated story, my mother was sitting at a table in Gray's Drug Store with Mable Bryson and Pearl Clinton, two close friends. She nodded toward Bill Morris and said to them, "That is the man I'm going to marry."

After my father's death in 1970, my mother flew to Colorado Springs, Colorado, where I was pastoring a United Methodist Church and visited with me. During her visit I asked a number of questions about their early relationship.

She said my father asked very little about her past. She told him about going to college and her first job teaching at the Pinedale Elementary School near where her family had settled when they came to Mississippi. He did not ask, but she told him she was not seeing anyone seriously. She had had a number of suitors, all well-known to her family. She told him that her faith was important to her and that she disapproved of wild and riotous behavior. She said he listened.

Soon after that first date, Bill Morris was sitting on Joan Ferguson's front porch asking Jake Ferguson for his daughter's hand in marriage. To the best of my knowledge, the only other person present was my grandmother. They would have been sitting in the white wooden rockers. If they had been at home, I can imagine sisters—May, Ruby, Blanche, and Martha Glen peeking around corners whispering, "He's going to do it." I can envision my grandfather, rigid and unrocking, staring straight ahead at the two hickory trees and across the road as though he knew what was coming his way. It would have been early spring, a cool breeze and jonquils

Figure 14. Joan and Bill when they were courting

blooming.

Bill Morris was thirty-seven; Joan Ferguson was twenty-four. She knew his history. He had told her everything. She knew about his first wife, her problems with alcohol and drugs. His bankruptcy. His drinking. A car accident and the six months he had spent in traction. It is not known if she shared this information with others in her family. My granddad may have been more concerned about his daughter's suitor than his daughter: "She's a pretty girl," Jake said, "and smart but headstrong. You don't know her like I do. Do you think you can handle her?" My dad shared the question with me but never told me his response. At the time of that discussion with him, they had been married fifteen years. Obviously, in that interchange with her father, Bill Morris thought he could manage Josie.

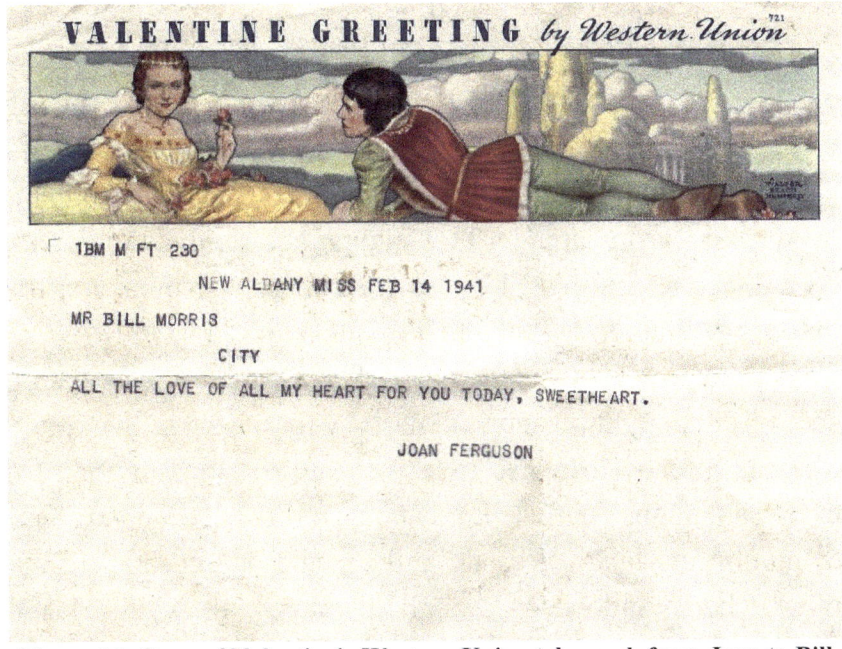

Figure 15. Copy of Valentine's Western Union telegraph from Joan to Bill

Within six weeks, they were married.

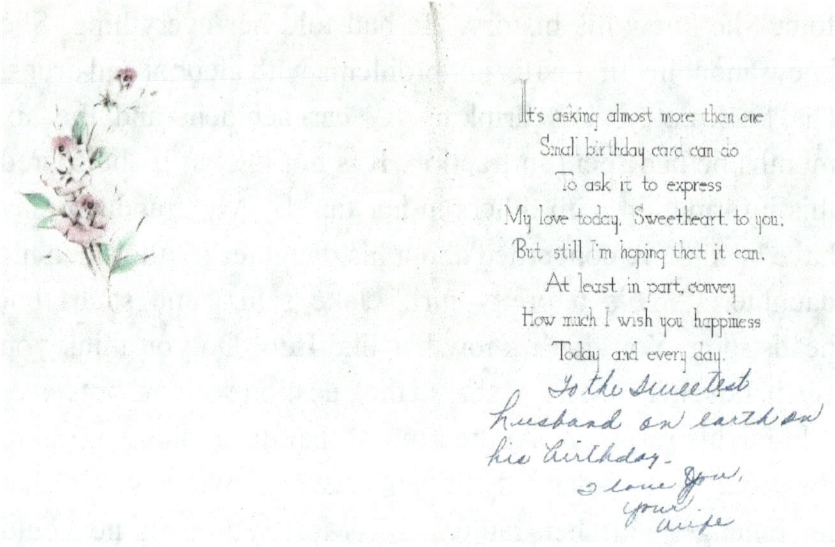

Figure 16. Copy of Joan's Birthday card to Dad on July 13, 1941, after their marriage

I will never forget my grandmother's comment on how quickly the relationship developed: "Time is for growing butterbeans," is all she had said and dismissed the issue, and the fact my father was thirteen years older than her daughter. My Uncle Byron came to the wedding and reminded my dad, "It's all about timing." I guess we expect watchmakers, the masters of time, to talk like that to one another.

I asked my mother one day, when I was seriously dating someone I thought I wanted to marry, why she chose my father. She had a ready response. "He was the best-looking man I'd ever seen, but he was also kind and generous, had a great sense of humor and laughed easily and…" She paused, looked out the kitchen window, as though distracted, then turned and looked at me. "And above all, he was patient." In later years, each time I recalled that statement, it carried greater weight and penetrated deeper.

I broached the same question with my dad. We were together on a fishing trip, just the two of us. We were sitting in his aluminum boat tied to a dead tree in the middle of Sardis Lake. I've always marveled how he could launch his boat, crank the motor and head straight for that one dead tree in what to me was an ocean forest full of dead trees. And we always caught fish in that spot. Perhaps, therein lies a parable.

It seemed a good place to ask the question. He responded, "My dad told me once to keep my eyes out for a woman with thin ankles and nicely shaped, tapered legs. He said if a woman had thin ankles and shapely legs that meant she was taking care of the rest of herself. And your mother is still as beautiful today as she was when she stepped into Gray's Drug Store."

I thought he was finished. He pulled up a crappie, hooked his mouth onto the stringer, put another minnow on his hook and dropped it back into the same place. Then, he looked at me and said, "My father also told me that choosing a wife was like walking between two rows of corn. You had to pick the best ear before you reached the end of the row," he paused, "and you couldn't go back." The metaphor of comparing an ear of corn to my mother was incongruous, but I got the point.

Joan Ferguson and William Edward Morris were married June 15, 1941, at the Methodist Church on Bankhead Street in New Albany by Reverend Oscar Scott. A year and a half later, they would be back at that chancel for my baptism by Reverend Scott. In attendance, beside my mother and father, were Grandmother Ferguson, Lena and J. D. Beard (godparents), Jamie and Paul Phyfer and infant son Jay, Mrs. D "Mama Dee" Daniel (later to be my dorm mother at Millsaps College), Mrs. Hugh Phyfer, Mrs. R. T. Smallwood and Mrs. Shannon Pitner.

Figure 17. 2 Photos of Mom and Dad in later years

Chapter 7: The War Years

I was born November 9, 1942. Roosevelt had declared war on Japan on December 8, 1941. Three days later, war was declared against Germany.

The very first memory I have of my mother, I was on a train with her and my father and many soldiers. I was an infant, so my memory is limited. But the smells I remember: the mixed aromas of cigarette and cigar smoke, beer, my mother's perfume. I recall seeing playing cards on a table and being handed back and forth over the back of a seat. I recollect flipping the pages of an animal picture book with a giraffe on the cover, my father's hand guiding me. I also remember my mother talking, and the soldiers listening to her. Looking back at photographs of her taken that year, I understand why she was the center of attraction.

Years later, my parents confirmed those recollections. It was indeed a troop train on its way from St. Louis, Missouri, to Memphis, Tennessee. My father was from Missouri. He, my mother, and I, had been to visit his family to introduce them to her and to me. The time frame, my mother said, was late 1944. I was almost two years old.

I have no memories of our first house. In my "Baby Book" my mother wrote it was the Old Bratton House on the corner of Cleveland Street and Adams Avenue. "We lived there 5 weeks and moved to a new home on Camp Avenue," the note said.

Figure 18. Joan, Bill, and Joe Edd

Figure 19. Bill and Joe Edd in stroller and Joan and Joe Edd in stroller, circa, 1943

Another two-year-old memory involved that second home and my Granddaddy Morris. I was in a swing in our backyard. The house is still there on Camp Avenue. I feel certain that was the house and the backyard because I later saw photos of a neighborhood Fourth of July parade along that street. My mother was pulling me in a wagon, and I was holding a small flag. Two older boys, Tommy, and Charles Hall, who lived next door, were in the parade. They were also who my mother called upon to catch me when I'd run out the front door, "naked as jaybird," the neighbors would say.

One more memory during the war years was of a tall, brown radio console. It sat in the center of the den, and each evening after supper (the evening meal was always called "supper," not "dinner." Dinner was lunch.) my father and mother sat around it listening to the news, which was mostly about the war. I remember lying on the floor and listening to two black men (Amos and Andy), Fibber McGee and Molly and a man I later knew as Walter Winchell ("Good evening, Mr. and Mrs. America and all ships at sea …") who spoke loudly and with urgency about the war.

In 1945, on January 14, my brother David Michael—was born.

Figure 20. Josie, David, and Joe Edd

Figure 21. Photos of David Michael

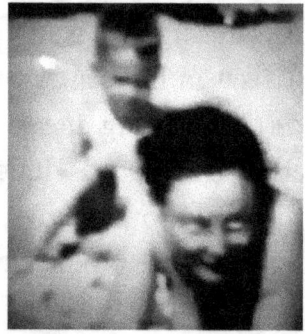

My mother had her hands full taking care of the two of us. Neighbors helped. Charles and Tommy Hall always pitched in, usually to track down one of us. Bill and Ed Smallwood were two of mother's other trusty babysitters. I recall standing in the front seat (no seat belts then) and riding around town in their pickup truck. I felt a deep sadness upon learning of Ed's death in a car accident below Sardis Dam.

My father was too old to be drafted. He was still manning his watch bench at Gray's. He had a strong clientele and was making good money. As he worked, an opportunity percolated in Josie's brain.

Chapter 8: The Jewelry Store

Before her marriage to Bill Morris, Josie had big ideas. She had dreams. She had listened to her husband's story of his first failed marriage, the jewelry store he had once owned, the bankruptcy, the indebtedness. She convinced Bill Morris he could have another jewelry store. He could start over. She would help.

They drove to Corinth and sought advice from his brother Byron who had a successful jewelry and watch business in a town the size of New Albany. Byron laid out a plan. Josie picked up where Byron left off and expanded the plan. Her brain, fueled by Lamar genes, brimmed with diamonds and jewelry, silver, crystal and fine china.

She and dad left Corinth with a blueprint, one that grew by leaps and bounds as they drove back to New Albany. They needed an outlet. Two stores up from Gray's Drug Store, an empty building became available. Bill and Joan Morris became tenants. Years later, Josie would buy the building.

To finance their venture, my dad obtained a loan from the Bank of New Albany. The president of the bank at that time, Frank Hall, believed in him. Josie was a big part of that positive impression. The amount of the loan is not known. Part of it my dad used to repay the debts incurred from his bankruptcy, reopening those doors to purchase merchandise for his new business—Morris Jewelry Store.

Josie rolled up her sleeves and went to work. She made several visits to Corinth. Byron educated her on the jewelry markets—Chicago, Dallas, New York, Atlanta—and loaned her jewelry, china, and sterling silver catalogues from Bulova,

Gorham, Royal Doulton, DeHaviland and Waterford, names I will always remember. Mom crammed. She took correspondence courses in gemology. She visited other jewelry stores in the area and gathered ideas about displays, showcases. She went to Memphis to Fargensteins, a wholesale jeweler, and spent hours with gemologists and jewelry experts, learning about diamonds, emeralds, and other fine gems. Later, she traveled to international markets, purchased her own stones, and designed her own rings, necklaces, and earrings.

The interior of the building had to be renovated. In that respect, Josie was gifted. Creativity ran in the family. Two older sisters, Ruby, and Blanche were a poet and a writer, respectively. Guy was an expert craftsman who could make anything. Dan knew how to inspire and motivate people. Robbie did for her husband what Josie was about to do for Bill Morris.

Josie could look at a room and tell you if it needed to be repainted, the colors to use, where furniture should be placed, pictures should be hung and how they should be artfully arranged. She turned that shell of a building literally into a showplace. She could flip a room, a house, or a building and decorate it in her mind before the first hand was raised. I think my mother could have flipped a town. In Batesville, her brother Dan did.

To my knowledge, this was my mom's first venture into interior decorating. To hear my father and others talk about her decorating ability, you'd have thought she had her Ph.D. plus twenty years of experience. Josie, ever the self-taught person, could do almost anything once she set her mind to it.

She roughly sketched a design for the store's interior—tall sliding glass window display cabinets for crystal and china along the west wall and standing glass-top showcases along the east wall for gems, diamonds, sterling silver, dinnerware. She and Dad reconnoitered and purchased used showcases from vendors in Memphis.

Dad's watch bench, the same he'd had all those years, was strategically placed at the front beneath the large clock he kept synchronized with the U. S. Official Clock in Washington, D. C. The railroad men, one of the reasons for his coming to the city, needed easy access to him as well as to the clock. Often, they stopped and idled their locomotive engines in the middle of town, between Bank of New Albany and Corner Drug Store, climbed down, made a dash to check their watches and then dashed back to the train. The cash register sat on a counter at the back of the store. This layout left room on the left side of the interior and rear of the store for something else. It did not take long for Josie, the entrepreneur par excellence, to fill it up with something else. That "something else" is the next chapter.

Morris Jewelry Store quickly became a bustling gathering place. Many came to set their watches. Others, to socialize. Preachers, politicians, and local businesspeople were regulars. Mom arranged a sitting area where "something else" would go later. My dad's winsome personality and Josie's flare and gift of gab quickly made Morris Jewelry Store a community magnet.

The ladies working for them added another dimension. From her "help" at home to her clerks in the store, my mother had an instinct for hiring good people. Most of the store clerks were relatives. One was a young black lady, Doris Knox. They were all hard working, loyal and engaging. Morris Jewelry Store was successful because of all of the above.

But Josie was the entrepreneur, the driving force.

Chapter 9: The Entrepreneur

Entrepreneurship was nothing new to the Ferguson and Lamar clans. Several had been movers and shakers, bargain, and deal makers. Beginning with their parents, their energy, sense, and calculation of the moment made things happen. The oldest, Guy, helped build and manage a logging empire in Jones County, Mississippi, and then transport it to Gilchrist, Oregon. Dan developed a sprawling Delta plantation, ran a funeral home, and served as mayor of Batesville, Mississippi for thirty-five years and was responsible for numerous civic improvements and innovative programs. Robbie married a Memphis businessman and helped him develop, expand, and manage his multiple enterprises. Following her husband Treadwell Aldrich's untimely death, Blanche took over a cattle farm and created a small fiefdom of houses and stores complete with an Episcopal Church in Michigan City, Mississippi, unleashing all of that energy while teaching and serving as a school principal at home and overseas.

Then there was Josie.

Jimmie Rogers remembers her first "experience" with Joan Morris. Jimmie was attending Blue Mountain College. She was taking home economics, when her teacher, Mrs. Hollis, told the class that, as part of a series of lectures, they had a special guest, a lady who had a jewelry and gift shop in New Albany. Jimmie vividly recalls the special guest:

> She entered the classroom with a suitcase and a box or two, and she was the most flamboyant wild personality when she spoke and had the most gorgeous

legs. She unpacked her things and talked about silver and china and crystal. I had never seen crystal. She also had a box of rings and watches. Afterwards, I couldn't resist. I would always go in her store when I was in New Albany.

Jimmie and son Ted worked for Josie in Morris Jewelry Store occasionally at Christmas.

Josie's multiple talents and realized dreams defy any chronological order. Nobody in New Albany was going to sell anything Joan Ferguson Morris couldn't sell. She transformed, morphed, that jewelry store into a revolving emporium.

The first addition to the store I recall was unlike anything imaginable for a jewelry store. But then again, that was Josie, doing the unimaginable. I went to the store one afternoon after school to wash the windows and sweep the floor, my weekly chore as part of my allowance. Something was different. Not just the sweet smell that hit me when I opened the front door, but two huge additions at the back of the store. My dad explained to me that they were refrigerators and that I was smelling flowers. Atop one of the huge refrigerators was a large sign: THE FLOWER BOX.

I had heard nothing about THE FLOWER BOX or gleaned anything from discussions between my mother and father. At the time, there were two flower shops in New Albany, enough to service the three funeral homes, multiple churches and regular customers needing flower arrangements for holidays and special occasions. Josie feared competitors getting wind of her venture and having sales events the day of her opening.

I knew my mother loved flowers. On reflection years later, I knew my love for flowers and gardening was probably genetically instilled, if not from osmosis, stemming from my mother and her mother and as far back as the genealogy stretched. Later, I had learned that my mother had checked out books from our county library on floral arrangements and that she had visited florists in nearby towns, especially in Oxford where one of her best friends, Kate Baker, owned a fashionable dress and gift shop. Josie had also set up an account with a wholesale florist in Memphis.

I do not recall how long The Flower Box lasted, a couple of years at least. The additional work to my cleaning job, having to sweep and gather all of the clipped stems and leaves, seemed endless. I am also unsure the reason The Flower Box folded. One day I entered the store to perform my cleaning chores and the two mammoth refrigerators were gone, the sweet smell with them. My mother was high octane and became easily bored.

She would not allow herself to be bored for long.

My junior year in high school, a lady named Mary Ann Mobley was crowned Miss America. The following year, another Ole Miss coed, Lynda Lee Mead, received the coveted award. Josie delighted in noting that the pillbox hat Lynda Lee wore in Atlantic City was purchased at The Hat Box.

That's right.

Hats.

Where the refrigerator units had stood were shelves displaying fashionable hats. Large wide-brimmed hats. Short-brimmed hats. Hats with wild plumage. Berets with feathers. Plain hats.

Anyone who knew Josie, could have guessed she would be selling hats. She was known for the large assemblage of hats she owned and wore. She and her sister, Blanche, were "hat ladies." Blanche had a large assortment from her worldly travels. Hats and travels quickly developed into a rivalry which would follow my aunt and my mother into their last days. When Josie died, her funeral was about the "hat lady." Following her death, a number of her hats were donated to the Union County Historical Society Museum where they remain and, at times, are on display.

Jimmie Rogers recalls Josie joining her for a trip to Anchorage, Kentucky, near Louisville. Jimmie was going to attend the wedding of the daughter of fellow New Albany native, Betty Jo Wicker Gaba. The ceremony was a grand occasion. "Josie wore one of her big broad-brimmed hats," Jimmie said, adding, "and it was a hit." It seems she and the hat made such a hit that Betty Jo asked if she could borrow six of my mother's "most ornate hats," for a function several years later that my mother did not attend. Jimmie, who was present and a member of this women's group, took six of Josie's hats. She commented, "Josie may not have been physically present. But she was *there*."

"The Hat Box" venture also seemed more manageable. Hats did not require refrigeration, which had cut overhead, mainly utilities. They did not need special storage and personnel for cutting, shaping, and making arrangements were unnecessary. Hats were simple. Boxes were opened, and the hats were removed, priced, marked and displayed. My cleaning job was easier.

I left for college and did not keep up with the side business. For a couple of years, on visits home, the hats were still there at the back of the store. I said to my father "Dad, what's next?" He winked and said nothing.

My freshman year had been at Ole Miss, and in 1961 I had

transferred to Delta State College. I was farther away from New Albany and did not go home often. But the first time I did, the first thing I saw as I was walking through the front door of the store stopped me in my tracks. I could see my mother selling flowers. I could see her selling hats. But I could not see her selling pianos, one right after the other, from mid-store to the back wall, a veritable and varied assemblage of the musical instruments.

My mother played the piano. She was not the only pianist in the family. Ruby played an organ that was in her parents' earliest home at Etta. Though I never heard her play it, Blanche had a piano in her home. I do recall an old up-right with yellow keys in the Marshall Hill Ferguson home, in the living room to the right just inside the door. As I write, and my mind drifts back to those days, I remember my mother, perched atop that rickety revolving stool banging out one hymn after another.

Selling pianos! How did she pull it off? The wheeler dealer, Josie contacted music stores in Memphis and Tupelo and arranged for a consignment plan. I never knew the details.

The piano business lasted longer than the other enterprises. With her sense of the market, Josie targeted churches and organizations that needed pianos. She made piano teachers aware of her sales. The business was a success. Then, too, it faded like the others. Josie grew tired of pianos. For Christmas, my dad gave her an organ.

What was next?

There was a lull, a large empty space in the store. Josie had a low tolerance for empty spaces. She had fallen in love with antiques, antique furniture in particular, and antique shopping. Wherever she went—by this time in her life she was traveling abroad—she kept a sharp eye out for antiques.

In 1965, when I was in Scotland studying at the University of Edinburgh, she and Marjorie Houston paid me a visit. We gathered at Greyfriars's Bobby for lunch. Afterwards, up and down the Royal Mile and Princes Street, on Haymarket Street, they shopped for antiques. I tagged along. My mother seemed obsessed buying and shipping antiques. Like a scout, Miss Marjorie was always a few steps ahead. "Josie, here's something you'll like." Or "Josie, you've got to see this." And the evermore, "Josie, this is a steal."

I marveled at their nice fit, the collaboration between the two. Back in the days, Marjorie was my mother's teacher in high school and taught her Sunday school class. I thought, too, of what my dad was going to say when all of those items began pouring into the store, and she still abroad.

While in Scotland, the antique bug bit me. I began buying old books. I purchased a hundred-plus year-old Bible for a threepenny, or "thrupnee." I shipped it home to mother who immediately placed it in one of the store windows and sold it for one hundred-fifty dollars to W. T. Lamar for his funeral home. I would never see that kind of profit margin again until my mother decided to sell the jewelry store and have an auction. The highest margin of profit was not on any watch or diamond or any china. It was on the plastic Coca-Cola handle from the door to the bathroom. It sold for $150, to a lady who collected Coca Cola memorabilia.

Hand-in-hand with Josie's entrepreneurial skills was her exceptional business acumen.

Chapter 10: The Businesswoman

Joan Ferguson Morris was an astute businesswoman. She was the creative energy behind the establishment and management of Morris Jewelry Store. Her husband brought his own wisdom into play and called many of the shots, but Josie ran the store.

It would be an understatement to say that Josie liked fine things. She inherited those tastes from her mother who inherited them from her mother, that strain being passed along through the Lamar French genes. But she was also frugal, that thriftiness stemming from the Ferguson side of the family, all the way back to the Scots.

The Scottish frugal mentality developed in the 1700s due to a financial crisis that bankrupted the nation. The Scottish nobility had tried to emulate the successful colonial exploits of the Dutch, English, French, Spanish and Portuguese by establishing a colonial outpost in the country of Panama. This interesting bit of history is called the Darien Scheme, for the Gulf of Darien, in which twenty percent of Scottish nobility heavily invested only to lose everything, thereby devastating the Scottish economy.

Long before the collapse of the Darien scheme, Scotland was a very poor country whose people largely survived on oats, cabbage, peas, herring, and potatoes. The only practical way to climb out of poverty was to be careful with your money. Scottish businessmen were not known for their generosity until they had "made it." Andrew Carnegie was a prime example. The powerful Scottish kirk's emphasis against extravagance and wastefulness added to this development of frugality.

I got a taste of Scottish austerity when I was a student in that country. I could take only one bath a week and had to pay a shilling, roughly $.25, for it. If my lights were not turned off, I was scolded by the landlady.

Some who knew Josie and traveled with her might tell you she was a penny pincher and tightwad. From the stories many still talk about her, the reader can decide.

When Bill Morris was still alive, he and Collins Porter, Jimmie Rogers' husband at the time, drove Josie and Jimmie to Middleton, Tennessee, to catch the late-night train for Washington, D. C., and eventually, after a stay with M. J. Black, to New York City. Marjorie Houston flew ahead to the Big Apple to meet them. Josie and Jimmie went by train because Josie insisted it was cheaper. They also sat up the entire trip. Josie said sleepers were too expensive, so they saved $12 by sitting all the way. She and Jimmie had seats across from each other. When the train came to a stop, Josie instructed Jimmie to put her feet on the seat opposite her and pretend she was asleep in order to prevent anyone from sitting with them.

Twenty years after Josie's first European venture, Jimmie Rogers tells this story: The two had flown to New York City and stayed at the Yale Club, guests of Jimmie's son Ted. In a 1977 Toyota Celica, they drove to his apartment in New Haven, Connecticut and slept on pallets. Jimmie recalled Josie saying, "This isn't costing us a dime. I've always wanted to sleep on a pallet." Driving through the countryside the next day, they stopped at a roadside antique shop. Josie bought two sterling silver tea sets for significantly beneath the sales price, had them shipped home and sold them quickly for a nice profit.

Then this narrative from Margaret McGill Lane:

> Your dad had just died, and Joan was going to have to attend David's wedding in Switzerland alone. She asked me to go with her and somehow wound up with my whole family: mother, James, Jamie Sue, and me. Joan had a travel agent in Memphis draw us a lovely and complete itinerary. Everything from train schedules to hotels to sights to see was planned in a concise and orderly manner. However, as you remember, Joan's "bible" was Europe on $5 A Day. Once we got to Europe, she pretty much did away with the travel agent's work, and we traveled by the seat of our pants…the cheap seat of our pants. Joan always looked at Europe on $5, and we found a "better deal." I remember that we spent one night sitting upright on a train in order to save $6 each for a berth. The last port of call was London, where we had several nights reserved at the lovely and well-situated Russell Hotel on busy Russell Square.
> Arriving late afternoon, we had to spend the first night there, but after breakfast the next morning (it was included with the price of the bed), Joan found us rooms across the street at the inelegant (and cheap) Morton Hotel. We packed our bags once more and checked out of the fine Russell. I was SO embarrassed! We looked like hillbillies as we dragged our suitcases down the walk. As we got into the center of the crosswalk at that busy intersection Joan's suitcase burst

open, and all of her clothing blew into the street. Of course, Mother stopped immediately to help, and Jamie and I wanted to act like we didn't know either one of them. As usual, however, both Mother and Joan called us back, and we had to chase Joan's dirty (it's the end of the trip) laundry all across Russell Square! My 19-year-old self just wanted to die!!!

Back in London, a different time.

The year was 1998. Sandi and I had taken our three children to Scotland and had traveled through England via Stratford-upon-Avon to London to connect with Josie. The Bermendsey Antique Market I will never forget. Sandi and I had to arise at 3:30 a.m. to go with my mother to a flea market she had learned about. Some folk's ears are tuned for music. Josie did enjoy good music, but her ears were supersonically wired for any news about markets, sales, and deals. If market was whispered from across a large room, Josie heard it.

"Oh, it is fabulous," she said of the Bermondsey Antique Market, her eyes sparkling with bargains. "They have everything."

I have also never forgotten one episode in that flea market. Josie was bent over a collection of rings, eyeing them curiously, the elderly male vendor standing over her. She picked up one of the rings, held it up to the morning light striking through the trees on the large meadow. She placed two fingers over her right eye as she would do when using her movie camera.

"I think it's a blue diamond," she said.

"How do you know, Mum?" the vendor inquired.

"Because I know diamonds," she remarked smartly. "I sell them, too."

Standing there observing, I watched a scene I'd seen unfold before. Using intimidation as a bargaining ploy, she was setting the man up. A feeling of pity for him suddenly welled up within me.

"What are you asking for it?" she probed.

"One thousand quid, Mum." He whipped out a calculator, but she preempted his tabulation.

"That's about thirteen hundred U.S. dollars."

He finished his calculation. "That is correct, Mum."

"It's not worth that," she scoffed in her tight-lipped stern business manner.

I knew the hammer was about to fall.

"Two facets are not symmetrical," she continued, still holding the fingers over her eye. "And there is a slight crack in the core."

The vendor did not respond. He stood as though transfixed.

She brought her fingers down from her eye, the finger-over-eye gesture part of the process, and now looked at him with both eyes. "I'll give you two hundred fifty pounds."

The man sucked in a deep breath. "Seven hundred fifty quid," he countered.

After some dickering back and forth, my mother walked away with the ring for five hundred quid. I do not know the rest of the story. Sandi and I and children left mother and headed for Paris. But if my mother was true to form, and she almost always was, she took that ring back to the jewelry store in New Albany and sold it for at least twice what she paid for it.

That memorable scene was not an isolated event. Josie was one shrewd businesswoman. She used a phrase in those years that is currently considered impolite, uncomplimentary, and politically incorrect. So, in deference, and out of respect for our Jewish friends, I'll use the word "dicker." She could dicker down, wear down, talk down anybody ... even her own children.

One of my early jobs was washing the jewelry store windows. Dad provided the bucket, the ammonia cleaning fluid he used on his watches, a brush, and a squeegee. I had been washing Mr. Lowrey's windows, two doors up, for a dollar. When dad offered to pay me the same wage, mother was standing within earshot (her earshot was long distance).

"Bill, don't pay him that. It's worth fifty cents."
After some dickering with him, they agreed upon seventy-five cents, my father always the compromiser, a behavior not in my mother's repertoire. After I'd finished the job, he slipped me the extra quarter and a wink that said, "Don't tell your mama."

But my father was not there that day in London, and the poor Brit was in no mood for a struggle with Josie. She got what she wanted and at her price. At that same flea market, I was interested in a soft-boiled egg kit, two small cups on a stand with matching tiny spoons. Standing nearby, my mother over-heard the transaction.

"You're not going to pay that much," she commanded.

I looked on embarrassed as she bartered that poor chap down. I bought it for half-price.

She haggled with the large companies from whom she and my father bought jewels, china, and crystal. In Victoria, Canada, I was there when she talked a lady down from two hundred dollars to seventy-five on a mohair coat that may still hang in her closet at home.

She dickered with servers in restaurants. "Is it fresh?" How many times have I heard that? If the server (waiters they were called back then) said it was frozen, she would request an adjustment in the bill. She did the same at nurseries with flowers and plants.

Josie could spot a bargain before it became a bargain. She could sense a bargain when it was a seed before becoming full bloom. She was a shopper's shopper, and when it came to striking a deal, she took no prisoners. Merchants who knew her sent out the underling sales corps to deal with her. In her wake of business travels, she left innumerable exhausted, frustrated, head-scratching and defeated retailers. She, also, left them remembering, "That tough customer from Mississippi."

Following my father's death, questions were raised about the store. Josie answered them quickly: she was keeping it. The watchmaking income was gone, but not entirely. She continued taking in watches for repair, farming them out to a few trusted watchmakers in Pontotoc, Tupelo, Ripley, and New Albany where one of their friendly competitors agreed to assist. I am unsure how the system worked, but she managed the watch repair flow and garnered a percentage.

At some point, Josie decided to sell the store and have a going-out-of-business sale. The prospective buyer was a Swiss man named Ziegfried Sollberger. My brother David, an attorney, handled Ziegfred's immigration papers, and Thad Cochran's office assisted. The entire affair was complicated. Josie had her going-out-of-business sale, but Ziegfred could not follow through on his part of the deal. My family became concerned, and David hired a detective in Switzerland to investigate Ziegfred.

The Swiss detective reported that Ziegfred's assets had

been repossessed by the bank. "He was dead broke," reported David. Les Sumner's, our family attorney, presented the findings to the New Albany attorney representing Ziegfred. Since Ziegfred had no money, the negotiations were dropped, and Josie resumed ownership and operation of the store.

However, there was a problem. Josie had already had a going-out-of-business sale. Mississippi law states a proprietor cannot have a liquidation sale unless the business is, in fact, closing. Morris Jewelry Store became Morris Brothers' Jewelry Store.

Morris Brothers' continued for a few years and then Josie decided it was time to close and have another going-out-of-business sale. She had an auction. It was held in an auction house in the middle of nowhere between Tupelo and Fulton. Priceless stones went for almost nothing, but Josie was ready to move on.

Her prior work and experiences with antiques took a different turn. She started a new business: Joantiques. She sold antiques from her home, which was already a museum, and leased booths at George Watson's and The Red Door. She continued to sell diamonds and jewelry, but she wasn't finished.

Her business card read—at the top—ANTIQUES-INTERIOR DECORATING-TRAVEL CONSULTANT. Below was her professional signature: JOANTIQUES and beneath that, Joan Morris. At the bottom was her home address and to the side her phone number and the hours: 11:00 a.m. till 5:00 p.m. *Evenings by Appointment Only.*

ANTIQUES • INTERIOR DECORATING • TRAVEL CONSULTANT

Joantiques

JOAN MORRIS

401 CLEVELAND STREET
NEW ALBANY, MISSISSIPPI 38652

601-534-6108
11:00 A.M. TILL 5:00 P.M.
EVENINGS BY APPOINTMENT ONLY

Figure 22 Josie's Business Card

I chuckle every time I look at the card. Anyone who has known Josie knew that she enjoyed staying up late at night and sleeping late in the mornings. Her nights were her noons. Some days she would not arrive at the jewelry store until noon or later. On many nights, my dad had to sleep in another bedroom so he could arise early, be at work before eight to open the store and take the expensive merchandise out of the safe to display. Often, he went to the store earlier to get watch repair work completed before customers and the railroad men with their timepieces began arriving.

I still have some of those business cards. Writing this, I smile to myself at what's on my business card: Psychologist, Jury Consultant, Author.

Josie knew how to make a buck.

She also knew how to invest a buck.

My brother and I were aware our mother and father had been investing. When dad died in 1970, she continued investing. Not one to put all of her eggs in one basket, she diversified. She was into buying and selling not only stocks but also bonds. After her death, reviewing her papers and investments with the Bank of New Albany, we discovered she had more investments than we had imagined.

Josie threw nothing away. Sifting through the ton of papers she left, we found a wealth of records. Some were on ledgers, some notes on the back of Fargonstein envelopes: bought this ring for $560 on 10/24/81, sold it for $950 on 12/15/84. These notes were everywhere: files, ledgers, some just lying loose in a shoebox. She paid great attention to detail, left nothing untouched, no stone unturned.

She kept immaculate records, documentation of each and every payment my father made toward resolution of his bankruptcy, something he had incurred and had initiated before they met. She kept documentation of each deposit she made in the Bank of New Albany of payments to her from Zeigfried Sollberger, payments toward the sale of her business, checks that turned out to be fraudulent.

On contract bridge scoring pads, she kept record of individual scores. One has Jerri, 3410; Betty, 140; M. A., 140 and Josie, 1120. I came across a copy of the SBA loan "Satisfaction of Security Investments" document dating back to 1985 when she purchased the store. She kept records of every payment, noting the identity of each document or item. If she removed money from petty cash, she made note of the withdrawal and recorded when she returned the money. It is not unusual that she made these meticulous notations. Others do it all the time. It is remarkable, and a testament to her business acumen, that she *kept* them ... all of them. These records were not for someone to see and write about her later. But in the business world, this process was prudent. The practice was also pure Josie, businesswoman *par excellence*.

Chapter 11: Renaissance Woman

According to the *Collins English Dictionary*, several meanings are given for the term "Renaissance man:"

"A cultured man of the Renaissance who was knowledgeable, educated or proficient in a wide range of fields."

"A present-day man who has acquired profound knowledge or proficiency in more than one field."

"A man of any field who has a broad range of intellectual interests."

The one that caught my eye was this interpretation from Leon Battista Alberti (1404-1472), an accomplished architect, painter, classicist, poet, scientist, and mathematician who boasted of his skill as a horseman and in other physical feats—"a man that can do all things well that he will."

A woman can do all things well, too. And Joan Ferguson Morris was one of them. Granted, it would be a stretch to say she was a scientist, mathematician, skilled horseman, etc., etc. But she had her own catalogue of accomplishments.

Where do I begin?

I could go back to a small country farm, with parents and parents before them who were determined and persistent dreamers. I could continue through the early years of a vibrant and, at times, recalcitrant and defiant youth, flashing her beauty and brains. I could take us through her college days at Delta State and Hinds Junior College. I could explore more of her early personal history where gifted foundations were surely being laid. But I go back to a man named Bill and a store named Morris Jewelry, for that was when Josie began coming into her own, when all of that accumulating creative energy exploded.

My mother's renaissance, rebirth, began, I believe, when she met my father. Not later when they dated and got to know one another. Not when they became engaged, and he sat on her front porch and asked Jake Ferguson for her hand in marriage. Not on June 15, 1941, when they said their marital vows in the New Albany Methodist Church. Not on their honeymoon. But on a day in December of 1940, when she walked into Gray's Drug Store. That's when the fire fell, when the energy flared, and the dreams began percolating.

It all began with my father's dream of owning another jewelry store. Despite his failures and other personal issues, his dreams never died. He brought them with him to New Albany, Mississippi, to Gray's Drug Store … and to Josie.

You have read of the energies and thoughts she poured into that venture, how it spurred her to take correspondence courses in interior design, to master knowledge and design of fine gems and stones (my brown-star sapphire she purchased in Bangkok and designed the mounting … I still have the ring), become a first-class entrepreneur and expand Morris Jewelry Store many times over, giving it a greater depth and breadth than just a jewelry store but also a diversified fine gift shop.

There was, also, an artistic side of my mother I had never fully appreciated until after her death. I had almost forgotten that she was an accomplished pianist and later an organist. How could I forget the harp she purchased, set up in the living room and learned to play, or the accordion, strapping that huge instrument through her arms and playing, not just the white keys, but also the tiny black buttons on the side, and at the same time expanding and closing the billows. She tried the flute. Our band director, Jimmy Hanry, worked with her, but he said she never quite got the breathing down. When he told me that, I could not conceive of my mother not "getting her breathing down."

I was in the New Albany High School band and played drums. One day, I brought home a snare drum to practice. I was in the back of the house and thought my ears were deceiving me. Surely, I was not hearing drum rolls. I walked into the living room where I'd set up the drum, and, to my disbelief, my mom was stroking drum rolls, a skill that took me months to learn.

She had a beautiful soprano voice and sang in the choir at the Methodist Church. The times I stood beside her holding the same hymnal and singing, the rich vibrato voice I heard was soulful and passionate.

Josie was intensely competitive. Weeks before Christmas, she applied her creative right brain into decorating the house, inside and out. She was doing this for herself, but she was also competing for the best house Christmas decoration award. It was not important that the house looked Christmas perfect. It was not important that people oohed and aahed and told her how beautiful her decorations looked. It was not important that she thought so, too. It was important that she won.

On an unannounced night—and Josie had ways of knowing the exact date—mysterious judges drove through New Albany and decided on the winners. If my mother knew the identity of the judges, she never said. I would not be surprised that she knew their names, the towns from which they came and the names of streets on which they lived, so thorough, complete, and impassioned was her research, *investigation* perhaps the better word. *Surveillance* another. She had friends planted around town tracking the judges. Each block, each house they passed. Timing was everything. The "Best Decorated House" contest was a BIG deal.

I don't know how many times she won the coveted prize. I do recall one. She had Boy Scout Troop 18, in full uniform, wearing white choir capes, singing on queue when her "spies" told her the judges were coming down Cleveland Street. I still have the black and white photograph. Our Scout Master Les Sumners, also in full uniform, directing. The scene was something to behold, my mother peeking through the living room curtains as the judges drove by.

Figure 23. Christmas Scout Choir

I've already noted her interior decorating ability, the notation on her business card. She had a keen, intuitive sense of what worked—colors, furniture, enamel, molding, wallpaper. I wish I had pictures of our first house on Cleveland

Street. It sat back from the street; the short wrap-around columned porch elevated. She morphed it through several remodeling phases. At the time, as a child, I did not see anything being remodeled. All I saw was something being torn down and rebuilt. The house, as it stands today, has little or no resemblance to the first house. Another interesting note about the house on Cleveland Street: It was Bill and Nan Rutledge's first home.

Josie loved paintings, artwork. A few years before her death, she began taking art lessons. Some of her paintings are worthy of display and hang in my office. For several years, she painted watercolors and oils. Her paintings reveal a soft touch.

I have saved gardening until last. I had always known she worked in the yard, but her love for plants, flowers and vegetables did not become apparent to me until I started gardening. I was working on my doctoral dissertation. Growing vegetables and flowers around my small apartment in Oxford, Mississippi, provided a balance for the more reclusive life of reading and typing. My mother would visit me, note what I was doing and began sharing the wisdom of horticulture passed down from her parents. Giving me a guided tour of her gardens when I visited offered a softer, gentler side of my mother. In those moments, I felt closer to her.

Writing about my mother's talents, hobbies and avocations makes me wonder how she achieved all that she did. In retrospect, the answer is simple. Stately and regal, with a flourish of the dramatic, Josie was, at her core, a Renaissance woman.

Chapter 12: Brown v Board of Education

On May 17, 1954, *Brown v. Board of Education* hit my world. A little girl courageously opened a door for her people and others to follow. In retrospect, I know the story well. Then all I knew from the news on television was that a "colored" third grader named Linda Brown, who lived somewhere in Kansas, had to walk one mile through a railroad switchyard to get to her elementary school even though a white elementary school was only a few blocks away. Her father tried to enroll her in the white school and was turned down.

Brown v. Board of Education is familiar to all of us now. At that time, I ask my mother what *"versus"* meant and she said it meant when two people or groups were playing, one was against, versus, the other. One thing led to another, and the case landed in the Supreme Court. Chief Justice Warren Burger read the decision of the unanimous court, a decision that forever changed my life and the lives of every Southerner, black and white.

New Albany, like other Southern towns in those days, was racially divided. There were separate drinking fountains and separate restrooms. Separate houses of worship. Separate funeral homes. I knew the "colored people," as I referred to the African American population back then, had a separate entrance to the "picture show" and sat on one side of a partitioned balcony. I knew there were restricted areas where colored people could live. Today we refer to them as ghettos.

But I lived on a block that was not divided, where there were no partitions. A block where there was a white doctor on one side and a colored beauty parlor out his back door on the other; a block where the colored help lived among their white employers, where a white woman (my mother) and an older colored woman worked the same garden on the small plot between their houses.

I also knew that in our house on Cleveland Street there was a genuine kindness, regardless of color, for human beings. My father was kind to everyone. Poor folks, white or colored, would pick up their fixed watches and he would say, "No charge." Each spring, just before Easter, he went down to Taylor Men's Store, chipped in with other merchants, and bought Wes Schooler, a black town sports mascot, a pair of wingtip shoes and new suit, complete with a silk tie and silk handkerchief for his coat pocket.

My mother belonged to the Women's Society of Christian Service and would come home from their meetings telling my father how Miss Marjorie (Houston), their leader, said colored people were children of God just like us. I was standing by my mother in Goldsmith's Department Store in Memphis one day when a lady told her "Colored people" were trying to destroy our Southern way of life, and my mother told her, "In heaven, there is no Southern way of life."

While the country was waiting for racial justice, Joan Ferguson Morris was ahead of her time. Long before *Brown vs. Board of Education*, she was enacting it, building bridges for others to cross. Jake and Susie Belle Ferguson had imbued all of their children with a sense of racial justice and kindness to others, regardless of their color, creed, or origin. A similar strain of fairness ran through the Lamar branch of the family. L. Q. C. Lamar, the famous silver-tongued senator from Mississippi (mentioned in J. F. K's *Profiles in Courage*) who, as it was passed down to me, freed his slaves before the Civil

War erupted. I don't know if the story is true. But the fact the anecdote was inborn and part of Ferguson/Lamar lore, transmitted along that genealogical grapevine, attests to a larger significance. People of color were treated with dignity and fairness on both the Lamar and Ferguson side of the family.

My mother's attitudes toward blacks surfaced in my life in one vignette after another. A few are worth sharing.

Lula was one of our first maids. I did not know her last name until later in life. She was dutiful and responsible and generous. She lived on a street with a special name, an interesting piece of New Albany history.

I grew up in an area of town called "the North Side." Most of the streets were named for presidents. As a teenager, I rode my bike down to the GM&O railroad tracks, where the streets of North Side began, and followed them north, noting the names of the avenues as I went: Washington, Adams, Jefferson, Madison, Monroe and then Jackson which bordered the west side of the block where I lived.

I recalled that the next street, on the other side of that block, was not named for a president, but for someone named Peterson. After Peterson, the names of presidents picked up again—Van Buren, Harrison, Tyler, etc. At Polk, I turned around and rode back down the hill and stopped. Peterson. A two-block street named for someone named Peterson. I had memorized the names of the presidents in sixth grade. Or had I? I pulled out my *World Book Encyclopedia.* No president named Peterson. My father and my mother had no idea why the street was named Peterson, nor did anyone else I queried. However, I felt compelled to find out. Surely there was a story behind the name. I never solved the mystery, and over time, as

I grew older, the intrigue slipped from me.

Years later, one of my heroes, a man I revered, knew I was writing a novel set in New Albany. One day, he handed me an article he had cut from the local *Gazette* and said, "You might find this helpful." The piece was entitled, "Do You Remember 'Aunt' Rose Peterson?"

Do you remember "Aunt" Rose Peterson? "Aunt" Rose was reportedly a former slave of about one hundred years old. About the middle nineteen twenties, she was the cleaning lady for the Bank of New Albany. Each day she would walk to the Bank, after closing time and perform her duties and then walk home coming up Cleveland Street. She wore long dresses and was rather heavy and wore an old worn-out scarf and large men's Brogans. She also had difficulty walking and used a heavy wooden cane. All of the kids in the neighborhood would wait for her at Jackson Avenue and ask her each day if she had anything to give them. Her usual answer was "Get outta here chilins. Ain't got nothing for you." She would wave her heavy walking cane in a threatening manner, and all of us kept our distance. She would plod on a few more steps and stop and reach in her big old cloth bag and pull out a small piece of candy and one by one would call at us and hand us a candy and say, in her gruff voice, "Now, get outta here." She was so well known and highly thought of that the Board of Aldermen changed the name of the street one block east of Jackson Avenue to Peterson Avenue. "Aunt" Rose lived in the house that still stands directly behind the house on the northeast corner of Cleveland and

Peterson. I remember "Aunt" Rose!

The article was written by William ("Bill") Devan Blizzard. He and his two sisters, Ruth, and Jean were in high school with my mother. Ruth was one of my mother's best friends. Life is interesting, how things seem to come full circle. Bill Blizzard came back into my mother's life and became her companion in her last years.

Back to Lula and the thread of that story. Aunt Rose and Lula Peterson were related. Lula lived in that same house. She was our "help." Later in life, in seminary pouring over biblical texts, I kept coming across that word "help." It was not good that man should be alone, so the Lord made, "him a help meet for him" (King James Version). In Psalms the Lord is "our help and our shield" and "a very present help in trouble."

That was Lula Peterson. Regardless of the weather, she trekked up the street named for someone in her family and through our next-door neighbors' back yard, through howling winds, blowing debris, and falling limbs. I remember the ice storm of 1948. I was six years old. I recall the long icicles hanging from the roof, loud booming sounds of tree branches breaking and crashing. The power was out for days. We lived in the back den where we had a gas heater that kept us warm, and we slept on pallets under piles of quilts.

The first day of the storm, I remember my mother pulling on her goulashes, and my father asking her, "Joan, where are you going?"

"I've got to warn Lula. There's a line down and she might step on it."

Tree branches booming like cannon salvos and breaking all around her, from a den window I watched my mother pick her way through fallen limbs, wind her way around the Poe house next door, stop and wait at the edge of the street. I heard her shout and saw her wave. A few minutes went by, and Lula joined her, and they walked together back to our house to the duties that awaited Lula, our help.

Lula stayed the day. She cooked and cleaned while all of us huddled in the one room with heat. At the end of the day when she was finished, I crawled up to the window again and watched her make her way back home, back through whatever mush or ice or fallen debris covered the ground to her little house. I saw the smoke from her chimney begin to wriggle up the sky and took comfort that she was helping herself before she, too, went to bed and her lights went out.

In that ice storm, my mother may have saved Lula's life. When Mother died, it was Lula's niece in that hospital room who grabbed and held me.

There were other instances, acts of acceptance and kindness to blacks. This one memorable for all time.

David Wade, forever and ever it seemed, was our gardener. He was black as nile dirt, never changed clothes and smelled like he never bathed. He wore a khaki shirt and pants four sizes too big with suspenders and a tattered felt hat where the sweat stains ran out to the rim. In winter, he wore rubber army boots, and in the other seasons old shoes with the toes cut out, sole and all, so his toes hung out.

He spoke in a raspy whisper, as though each word hurt and came from a special pain. His false teeth clattered slightly so his speech had a rattling effect, along with the mumbling, which made him sound like he was struggling. David Wade always talked to himself while he worked, whistling every now and then, familiar tunes I had heard in church.

Lula, who lived near David Wade, entered our house one morning very upset. I was at the store washing the front windows and sweeping. My father received a call from my mother. At the time, I did not know what she said to him, but he told me to drop what I was doing and go with him. I remember it was fall and cool outside because in the rush, I'd left my coat in the store.

My father was an unhurried man, but that day he scratched off when he let out the clutch and the car shot out of the alley into Main Street like a fire truck. We passed stores so fast I couldn't read signs I'd seen a thousand times. He went through traffic lights and stop signs, honking his horn all the way. I asked him why we were rushing, and he said David Wade might be dying. "Lula came to the house and told your mother."

David Wade lived down the street from Lula in a small dirt-floor shack bordered by privet hedges. Lula was in a frenzy in the street waiting outside of the privy hedge. My father asked Lula to wait outside, that we would take care of David Wade. His voice was firm but kind. It must have helped her. She seemed to calm down, all but her hands, which kept up a flutter on her apron.

I followed my father through a narrow break in the privet hedge to the small shack whose roof I'd only seen from a distance, a hut cobbled up out of a confusion of boards and shingles and cardboard. The door was low and my father, as short as he was, had to stoop to get in. I stooped, too, and stepped down onto a dirt floor. The only light came from a small screenless window and long cracks along the walls. The air felt dead, smothered by the dark and the smells of woodsmoke, kerosene and mildew. It was an air nobody could feel good in.

My eyes adjusted quickly to the dark, and I saw my mother tending to David Wade who was lying on a single sheet of plywood atop two sawhorses, a rolled-up towel beneath his head. My mother standing over him dabbing his forehead with a rag. Beside this makeshift bed was a ladder-back chair where I figured Lula had been sitting and watching over him.

My mother said, "Bill, it doesn't look good. He needs to go to the hospital."

I stood and watched as my father walked over to David Wade and slipped his arms beneath him, lifted him off the plywood and then carried him out to the car. My mother and I followed.

In those days, our hospital was small. To get to the emergency entrance, everybody went through the front door. Everybody that was white, that is. The blacks had a separate entrance and a separate lobby. My mother and I walked behind my father as he kicked open the front door and cradled David Wade in his arms through that lobby of amazed white faces. I heard somebody say, "Nigger lover," but my daddy didn't turn and look. Instead, he kept on through another set of swinging doors and down a long polished carbolized hall, our footsteps echoing off the shiny walls, and on through the swinging doors beneath the large red letters that said EMERGENCY.

No one in the emergency room seemed to be in a hurry to help. I will not tell you what my father said, the actual words, but they were bullets, and they weren't missing their targets. Before he was through, the triage nurse and her staff were stumbling over each other's feet to help. David Wade lived.

My mother stood beside my father as he paid the bill. We took David Wade home, but not to his shack. Lula had fixed a bed for him in her house, and she tended to him until he was ready to be back on his feet and return to gardening.

Years later, I was home from college and sitting at the small desk in my bedroom and gazing through the curtained window. Streetlights lining Jackson Avenue dropped pools of light onto the dark, wet pavement, and I saw a figure moving into that first lonely pool of light. It was David Wade, ancient of days, going home, to his shack behind the privet hedge, pulling his Western Flyer wagon, the measured click of its wheels as he went in and out of those illumined circles, like Jimmy Durante signing off, except David Wade never turned around and waved. I thought again of how my mother and father saved his life, enabling him to continue taking care of people's yards, including ours.

I cannot close this chapter without telling of one of my mother's finer moments. As Jimmie Rogers recalls the episode, she and Marjorie Houston and Josie had traveled by train to New York to attend the 1964 World's Fair, the year of the infamous "Summer of '64" in Mississippi, lynchings and church burnings and freedom riders. The three had been seated at a restaurant, one of the several surrounding the ice rink at Rockefeller Center.

"We were dressed up and had ordered our meals and glasses of wine. Our waiter, who was a nice-looking young man, said, 'Where're you ladies from?'"

"Mississippi," Josie spoke up.

"Is that where they sic dogs on niggers?" the waiter said.

Jimmie describes a deafening silence, followed by Josie

calmly laying her napkin on the table and saying, "Get up, girls. We're leaving."

"But you ordered, and you haven't finished your wine," the waiter said.

Staring right at him, Josie said, "We're leaving."

"And we marched out, Josie leading the way," Jimmie said.

Josie was a woman ahead of her time.

Chapter 13: Traveling Josie

Over a span of centuries, from the highlands of Scotland and the wine country of western and southern France, Fergusons and Lamars have been travelers. Their migration to this country continued until they hit a sweet spot in northeast Mississippi. Some, however, did not stop and kept moving on.

For Josie, the travel bug was a combination of genes, wanderlust, and adventure. If her families had no history of migration; if the Fergusons and Lamars had stayed in Scotland and France, Josie, with a low tolerance for boredom, would have roved. If there was no excitement in her life, she created it. She traveled.

I recall the first trip our family took. I remember it was winter because I was in the first grade, and my mother had obtained permission to take me out of school. We went to Florida. Based on mother's filming of our trip, we were gone about two weeks. She was one of the first in New Albany to own a movie camera and projector, the ancient type with the two large upper and lower wheels that threaded the film across the light bright as the sun.

I still have the camera. Mom would be proud to know that it still winds and unwinds. I can see her now, placing a finger over her right eye, sighting with her left and pushing a button that caused a little whirring sound. Several years ago, I had DVDs made of the movie reels. Occasionally, I play the disc and enjoy seeing home movies that date back to 1948—movies of the ice storm of that year, the Tallahatchie River flooding along lower Bankhead Street and the Jockey Yard, tornado aftermaths, train wrecks and fires. Josie was a born journalist.

She had an enormous need to be in the middle of the action, whatever and wherever it was happening. She would have made a fabulous camera woman for a television station or movie producer.

There were no interstate highways then. On a trip to Florida, we probably traveled through Birmingham to the Gulf Coast and across to our first stop, Saint Augustine. Mother kept telling my brother and me that it was the oldest city in America. I remember holding her hand and walking along the ramparts of the old Spanish fort.

From Saint Augustine, we drove to Sarasota where my Uncle Byron, Aunt Lola Morris and their daughter, Marta, had a summer home. That particular leg of our trip was a challenge for my loquacious mother. Uncle Byron and Aunt Lola talked nonstop. Fortunate for them, my father was always a good listener. The memory is still there, sitting on their living room floor with my brother looking up at my uncle and aunt. My father sitting and listening. My mother sitting ... and listening. That is the memorable part.

Besides being a watch craftsman, Byron was an artist. He is still noted for his bird and beach scene watercolors. I have three of his works, one he painted at age ninety-one, a boat moored in a lagoon. Another one is a winter scene of the home of Nancy Hawthorne King's husband's old country home in Corinth. A third, a haunted scene depicts the devastation of Hurricane Donna in 1960, a lone pelican atop a solitary pier post. During his life, feature articles appeared regularly in *The Commercial Appeal and Sarasota Herald Tribune*.

In addition to his artwork, Byron was an historian. He wrote the entire detailed history of the Sumerians, Akkadians, and Babylonians. Later in my life, while visiting with him in

Sarasota, he showed me the four-inch-thick manuscript.

The next stop on my mother's carefully researched and planned journey was at Bok Singing Gardens and Tower. I could not conceive of a tower that sang. But this tower sang.

How did my mother know about it? She read and researched everything. She knew of places that were unknown to many in New Albany and beyond. There was no Disney World then, none of the theme parks that dot the area now. The tower and gardens were in the middle of Florida, south of Winter Haven. They are still there today, lusher, and more beautiful than ever.

Our journey continued north along the shores of the Gulf of Mexico where we played on beaches and enjoyed the balmy weather, Mom's movie camera constantly whirring.

The second family trip occurred in 1954. Apart from the excursion into Florida, which we vaguely remembered, the trip out west our mom planned set for my brother and me a tone of exploration and adventure we would have for the rest of our lives.

I was twelve years, and my brother was ten. In a 1950 Dodge, our family embarked on an epic three-month journey through most of the states west of the Mississippi River and two countries—Mexico and Canada.

Our four door 1950 model Dodge did not have AC. We had a cooler we tried to keep filled with ice. My brother and I alternated sitting on it. At times, especially crossing the southwest Arizona desert, my father stopped at service stations, soaked cloth towels, and hung them over partially rolled windows.

We left New Albany early on a Monday morning. I

remember the moon was still up. We went up Highway 78 to Memphis and crossed into Arkansas. At Little Rock, my dad took Highway 67 toward Dallas and Fort Worth. It was important we go to Dallas and Fort Worth.

"Why?" I asked.

"To see Cud'n Emma and Cud'n Lee Morris," our mother said.

David and I looked at each other. "Who?" we both asked.

Rewind to January 28, 1864. My great-grandfather, John Harris Lamar, married Susie Ann Morris. Their ninth child was Susie Belle Lamar. There were Morris' on my mother's side of the family, but they did not come from Missouri.

Fast forward to the early 1900s to Etta, Rocky Ford and Pinedale, Mississippi, and the devastating weather during those years. A branch of the Lamar family headed west to Texas, settled in an area just north of Fort Worth and Dallas. There, Cud'n Lee Morris founded the town of Chico, still there today, population 1,009. The Fergusons made a living farming in better terrain. The Morrises, Cud'n Lee to be specific, struck oil. I wonder to this day what and where I might be if my grandfather had moved with the Lamar/Morris branch of the family to Texas. If they had, I guessed I'd be a Texan, maybe a wealthy one.

Cud'n Emma and Cud'n Lee were characters. Both were eccentric, wealthy, and flamboyant. Both had expansive personalities, laughed heartily, and loved to talk. Sound familiar? But there was an exception in the stack.

Cud'n Lee was very rich. Besides discovering oil, he built the town of Chico, owned its bank and only mercantile store. But he was not ostentatious. He did not flaunt his wealth. Mother remarked that he wore the same pants and shirt the entire time we were visiting, which was three days. The only hotel in Chico, which he built and owned, was a ramshackle clapboard structure with hitching posts across the front, creaking floors, and water-stained wallpaper. He and his wife Annie lived on the top floor where we had the privilege of spending the night, looking out our window at a scene of hitching posts, mule-drawn wagons, water troughs, wooden plank sidewalks and an oil well in the center of the square. I thought I had gone a hundred years back in time. I recall awaking the first morning, looking through the draped window and thinking I was back in the picture show in New Albany. Any second, the Durango Kid might ride up. Years later, watching the TV show "Dallas," I thought of Cud'n Lee, how he could have lived in a mansion, but instead chose a humble, simple dwelling.

In a beaten-up pickup truck, Cud'n Lee drove us across his sprawling multi-thousand-acre ranch dotted with oil derricks and huge storage tanks. He took us atop one of the storage tanks, opened a hatch and said, "Now, look down and take a look at liquid gold." It looked black to me, but he said it was "gold."

Leaving Fort Worth and Chico, we took one road that led into another, roads that did not seem to be roads. My mother, the queen of shortcuts, pointed them out with great authority. She had meticulously planned the trip, as she meticulously planned everything, including, at times, my life. She had maps on the dashboard, maps on the seat beside her and maps folded into the overhead visor. Dad had no maps. He drove as mother directed, a parable of that relationship ... most of the time. My dad usually did not question mother's navigating skills, but he did stop at one point. "Joan, are you sure this is right?"

At Lubbock, Texas, Mom directed Dad to turn right, that we were going to Amarillo. At Amarillo, we spent the night at a motel called The Alamo. I remember the front gate was shaped like the Alamo from the pictures I had seen, as were the several bungalows beyond it. In my mind, I questioned why we went north to Amarillo instead of going straight, which seemed more logical. (I had looked at a map, too.) But I said nothing.

Years later, I grasped the significance of the westward route we took from Amarillo. Mom called it the "Mother Road," one of the first highways built in the U. S., she said. Dad called it "The Will Rogers Highway." Regardless of its moniker and despite the drab featureless land, for my brother and me Route 66 was an entertaining stretch of road. We saw gas stations covered with signs; colorful diners, cafes, and drive-ins; theme motels like the Mohawk Lodge and Totem Pole Park; a Cherokee Trading Post and antique museums. At those, we stopped.

One eventful, everlasting memory occurred in Albuquerque. Mom had a tendency to be jittery, probably from all that energy and tension knotted inside of her. We had been driving all day, and all of us were "wired." My brother and I saw it. Our father saw it. When Mother finally saw it, she bolted backward and shouted in a hysterical (a word I didn't know then, but would learn soon after) voice, "Bill! Bill! Don't hit that neon sign."

"Joan," my father looked at her and said calmly. "It's the moon."

She seemed to collapse, and her head disappeared. Then she started laughing. We all commenced laughing. It was truly the biggest moon I had ever seen, and it did seem to boom up out of the bright lights of the main Albuquerque drag, right in front of us. I have seen many moons since, but never one that big, that memorable or that orange.

The next day at Flagstaff, Arizona, where Mother said there was a marvelous observatory where the planet Pluto was discovered (How did she know that?), we left Route 66 and headed to see the Grand Canyon and the Painted Desert, and something new in our lives began. New to us but not new to others long, long before us.

Abraham did it. So did Isaac and Jacob. From Noah on, people of *The Bible* erected altars to remember the places they had been. My brother and I, at our parents' encouragement, began buying decals and putting them on the rear car windows. We also bought pennants, many of which I still have. Souvenirs purchased at the Grand Canyon and a vial of colored sand from The Painted Desert remain in the same box I placed them in sixty-five years ago.

We continued through Phoenix further into the Arizona desert, where nothing existed except cactus. There were few gas stations. Dad kept a sharp eye on the gauge. It was going down. "We need to stop somewhere," he said. Finally, on the other side of Yuma, if Yuma could have another side, Mom with her binoculars spied a gas station. She also needed to use the bathroom.

An attendant came out to fill up the car. He told Mom the keys to the outdoor johns were inside. There were two outdoor johns, side-by-side neatly painted white. Mom emerged from the station house and entered one of the johns. The attendant completed filling the car and went back inside. We sat waiting for Mom. She came out of one john and entered the other. We waited longer. Finally, she walked to the car, a quizzical look on her face. She got inside and slammed the door.

"Anything wrong?" Dad said.

She tried to smile. "Well, I went in the first one and a voice below said, 'Madam, I am painting under this one could you please move to the other john?'"

I had never heard my dad laugh so hard and so long. The attendant returned to the car and apologized. He said, "Sir, it's kinda deserted out here, and that's the only entertainment I've been able to manage."

A good laugh by all.

We moved on along Highway 80.

At some point beyond Yuma, we entered, for the first time in all of our lives, a foreign country: Mexico. The name of the town was Mexicali. The streets and sidewalks were dirty and muddy, people spitting left and right. "Trashy," Mom said. Not once, but several times. "Trashy. Just trashy."

We passed many curio shops. I have a fond remembrance of one. We stepped through a narrow doorway through a curtain of beads and saw colorful blankets hanging overhead and souvenirs—beaded and silver bracelets, necklaces, and pennants—aligned on shelving along both sides of the narrow aisle. An older, gray-haired Mexican lady was in charge. Speaking to mother in broken but understandable English, she began palming her hand around her shop at beautiful rugs and pottery assortments—plates, glasses, cups, soup bowls.

That day, I observed my mother's bartering skills. I have no recollection of the lady's asking price on a shiny pottery dinner set. For a long time, she and my mother haggled. Walking away from that shop, my dad carrying the box, she bragged about how she got the set for half-price. We carted that box the rest of the trip home. I never again saw that set of

Mexican "china." It was quickly sold upon our arrival home.

Something else we purchased in that shop. I see them everyday walking through my study. While mother was dickering with the Mexican woman, I had picked up two things with handles that rattled when I shook them. My dad said they were maracas. My brother and I both wanted a pair. A small boy nearby helped us pick out the ones we wanted. I presume he was the woman's grandson and her helper. He was about our age, ten or twelve. He asked my father if we wanted our names carved on the maracas. My dad asked the cost and the boy said twenty-five cents for each set. Dad nodded.

The boy took out a knife from his pocket and proceeded to carve our names—JOE EDD and DAVID. Sitting on his haunches, bent over, his eyes very close to his work, he concentrated with great intensity, carefully moving the knife blade with precision. I thought of another image, someone else I had seen at his work, one of my father's that Norman Rockwell would love to have painted.

When the boy was finished, the names looked professional, as though carved by an expert. The young boy held out his hand and said, "fifty cents." Dad gave him two dollars. That was my generous dad, my mentor of giving to others. As I have previously mentioned, often in the jewelry store I would see the poor people come to get their repaired watches and hear him say, "No charge."

Mother was upset Dad had purchased the maracas for us. "Now we're going to have to listen to them the rest of the trip." The maracas did make it home. Every time I pass them lying on a shelf in my study, I think of that small boy, that young entrepreneur who won that day by not "dickering." I remember, too, that he could speak our language, but we could not speak his. I was determined that someday that situation would change.

On the way to Los Angeles, we stopped at a site my mother, ever the budding scientist—Renaissance woman—had researched and put on our itinerary. Some background is important. On my eighth birthday, she and my father gave me two gifts that would forever shape my life: an *Eigermeir Bible Story Book* and a telescope. One gift opened and expanded the inner world of theology and religion. The other opened my venturesome eyes to the outer world of an ever-expanding universe. Lying on my back in our backyard, I counted the craters on the moon and the moons around Jupiter and lost myself in the Milky Way.

So, when Mom said I was in for a treat as we pulled into the large parking lot of Mount Palomar Observatory, I sat in disbelief gazing at the large white domed structure and the mammoth 200-inch Hale telescope protruding through its opening. Mom had done her homework.

After a long upward climb to the facility and once inside, I heard my mother say in her authoritative voice to a uniformed man at the front desk, "I understand that this morning between nine and twelve o'clock the observatory is open to the public."

"Yes, Madam," he told her. My father paid the entrance fee, and we were directed into a large domed area, straining our necks and eyes to see the huge structure that resembled a prehistoric giant. My mother inquired of our guide if her two sons could look through the telescope. He told us that was not possible, but there was a telescope not far away at Mount Wilson, in the mountains north of Pasadena, built by the same man named Hale who had built the 200-inch Palomar telescope. Mom removed her note pad from her purse and jotted down the information. The next night we went to the Mount Wilson Observatory and were allowed to look through its lens. What I saw leaves my vocabulary bankrupt. I still close my eyes at night and see those magnificent heavens, wondering how God had made them.

My mother and father, like their parents, believed in education. And firsthand experience was the best education. Little did they know they were launching their two sons onto a world pilgrimage, taking their education to the next level and beyond.

Excitement was building. Ahead lay Los Angeles and Hollywood. The perennial planner, Mom had located the name and phone number of a personal guide who would show us the city. This was 1954. No Bing or Google. No Internet. No online directories. How she located the name and phone number, I have no clue. All I remember is that a tall, dark-haired, mustached man wearing a dark suit appeared in front of our motel in a black sedan. The next experience I would have of riding in a limousine was when we took our children to New York City, and I rented one for one evening to take us to the Four Seasons restaurant.

Our guide, whose name is long forgotten, showed us all of the sights, and some we didn't know were sights. A vivid visual memory recalls where we ate that night. It was in a restaurant with a gurgling stream flowing right through the middle. The next day we saw Walter Pigeon (a movie star I didn't know) playing tennis, the homes of many movie stars and Forest Lawn Memorial, the most beautiful cemetery I had ever seen. I kept wondering, how my mom knew about all of these places.

From L. A., we took Highway 1 to Santa Cruz to see my father's mentor and former watchmaking boss. Mr. Pennell showed us the town and worked with Mom and dad on jewelry and watch business while my brother and I played on the beach across the street from one of his two jewelry stores.

Up Highway 1 again, at San Francisco we saw the special places—Fisherman's Wharf, Chinatown, the little street cars.

Our first stop in Oregon was stunning Crater Lake, where we had a snowball fight in the middle of July. Next, was Gilchrist, the timber town my Uncle Guy helped establish and was named for his boss. We spent a week with him and Aunt Emma. My brother and I used much of our time trying to trap chipmunks in their backyard. We caught two of the cute little creatures. We wanted to take them home, but my mother said, "No! Absolutely not!"

My father joined in the effort on our behalf and pleaded with Mom. Under the guidance of my Uncle Guy, a small cage that would fit snugly in the backseat of our Dodge was constructed.

Chipmunks and cage in place, me sitting atop the cage, we headed next for Washington and a cousin's home on Puget Sound. Further north, at Seattle, we took a ferry to Vancouver Island and Victoria. This was the first time ever for any of our family to travel on a ship, albeit a small one.

A few years ago, Sandi and I returned to Victoria when we were on an Alaska cruise. The same quaint streetlamps with hanging baskets of colorful flowers were still there, along with the elegant Fairmont Empress Hotel and the throne-like chair my mother sat in when told Queen Victoria had once sat there. Josie looked regal in any chair and made any chair look royal when she sat erect and crossed her legs, especially if she were wearing a hat. And how did she know about the famed Buchart Gardens?

Then there were the shops … the shops … and more shops. And the bartering, purchases stacking up—mohair coat, diamond rings, necklaces, earrings. At disembarkation, my mother wore most of what she bought to avoid paying duties, including several rings. (The dollar went further in Canada). A lasting image was my father standing in a packed line to disembark the ferry, a package beneath each arm and holding several tied with hemp cord in his hands. Mom could not help him, she had to keep us. My dad couldn't put the boxes down. He just stood there in one place for the longest, my mother and brother and I looking on. My heart went out to him, to the look of pain on his face, not knowing the palms of his hands were bleeding. Not once did I hear him complain.

We departed Seattle, the car loaded with market items for resale at the jewelry store, souvenirs and two chipmunks which we had to keep watered and fed. Nothing of note or memorable occurred until we left Yellowstone National Park, had seen all the sights there including geysers, hot springs, buffalo, and Indians in full regalia, and were driving across a ho-hum barren stretch of Wyoming. Mom had the binoculars scanning for cops. Dad was pushing the speed limit, and we had two illegal chipmunks abducted from the state of Oregon. Then this: "Bill! Bill! Slow down!"

"Why?" he said. "There's only one car ahead of us, and it's way ahead."

Her eyes still glued to the binoculars, she said, "But that car looks familiar." She lowered the binoculars then raised them again to her eyes. "It's a station wagon … it's maroon."

"So," my dad remarked slightly irritated, his head tilted back as though he was rolling his eyes.

"It looks familiar," she said and then added, "The Bakers are vacationing in Wyoming. There are feet sticking out a back window. They look like William's feet. I'll bet you anything they belong to William. Speed up, Bill, and pass them."

As we sailed by the maroon station wagon, everyone gave surprise waves, including William with his skinny feet. How in the world? I thought then and still wonder now.

Colonel Bill and Kate Baker of Oxford and their children Virginia, Sandra and William were dear friends. Many Sundays we drove graveled Highway 30 to visit them, or they drove to visit us. They lived next door to the Faulkner mansion, Rowan Oak, and often my brother and I joined the Baker kids and played in the sprawling yard of the big house. On one occasion, we helped Faulkner catch a horse, and another time we helped him pull weeds, no knowledge at the time we were in the company of a great writer, whose stories, and books we would read years later.

A remarkable site we visited in Colorado Springs, Colorado, was Santa's Workshop. It was a theme park complete with Santa Claus (even in summer), reindeer, elves, deer, amusement rides, etc. Little did I know then that twenty years later I would become its manager.

The rest of the trip home was uneventful.

On that long western sojourn, my brother and I were the right age. We were impressionable. Nothing could top all that we saw and did as a learning and educational experience. Our small minds were like flypaper. The trip pre-pared and ensured us for more to come. Like our mother, we would become travelers.

Others learned that traveling with Josie could be illuminating, exciting and challenging. Margaret McGill Lane shares this story. She was on the same European jaunt mentioned previously. Margaret tells it better than I could:

> Then there was the language problem…in Germany, in Switzerland and finally in Italy. But language was no problem for Joan…she just spoke English using what she perceived to be the accent of the particular country we were in. The one that had us laughing about for years was "separatti check!" that she used all over Italy.

With the same group in Germany, Margaret again:

> Then there was the night in a German hotel when I blew the lights out of the entire wing of our hotel. I didn't know which adapters and plugs to use, so I asked Joan and Mother. Joan said the adapter wasn't necessary, so I just plugged my hairdryer in. Total darkness enveloped us, and the stench of burning wires was everywhere. Mother and Joan made me go downstairs to explain what had happened. When I arrived in the lobby, there was a multitude of Japanese tourists complaining (I think—I don't speak Japanese) that they had no electricity. Amid the chaotic uproar, I meekly told the manager that, "My lights are off, too…"

Perhaps the most hilarious event of Margaret's trips with

Josie occurred much earlier, in 1960, on a trip to North Carolina where they picked up Margaret at a camp. Josie, Lily Francis, and Margaret were traveling through Cherokee and stopped at an Indian village after they had been digging for rubies and sapphires. Margaret again:

> Joan needed to "sit a while" in the bathroom, but there was only a dormitory type of bathroom with one toilet. This toilet was enclosed in a stall but had only a sheet in place of a door. There were several of us standing in line, waiting for Joan to finish so we could have our turn. This old Indian woman, the first in line, got tired of standing and began to try to sit on what she thought was a post. It was Joan's knee, shrouded by the sheet. Joan screamed, and the Indian woman jumped, screamed, and ran out. The situation was all good. Joan decided she was finished and gave up her position, and the line had lost the one in the "next up" position…all good for the rest of us.

On a trip to New York City, Jimmie Rogers remarked on Josie's inventiveness while traveling when the handle on her luggage broke. Using a tube of lipstick, she quickly manufactured a new handle.

As I look back over my life, when it came to traveling, my mother was the dominant force.

If she and our father had not taken David and me on that epic journey out west, I wonder where our traveling lives would be. For me, and I think David would agree, that was when the bug bit.

Thank you, Mom.

Figure 24. Christmas mid-90's her home in New Albany

Figure 25. Christmas at our house

Chapter 14: Sarge

When our children—Meredith, Anna Katherine, and Jason—were still in elementary school, together they picked out a Christmas gift for Grandmama Josie, one that would match the nickname they had for her. They had talked about the gift and agreed. It was a secret they would not share with Sandi and me, but they wanted to go to an Army surplus store, and we had an inkling.

Grandmama Josie would not let her grandchildren chew gum in public, leave the kitchen without cleaning their plates or leave their bedrooms without making up their beds. She also did not let them eat junk food and the list, to them, was endless. In the Army surplus store, the kids had gone their separate ways. One of them spotted an item and called the others over to see it. I paid for it unseen. When we got home, they wrapped the gift, still a mystery, themselves.

That Christmas Day, we all sat eagerly around the tree in Josie's home, awaiting the moment she would open the neatly and colorfully wrapped gift. But it still lay there beneath the tree as if it were somehow forgotten. Finally, one of our children, I don't recall which one, could no longer stand the suspense, went over, and handed the present to her and said, "This is from us grandkids, Grandmama."

With a precise smile, my mother began carefully pulling the ribbon and tearing the paper. She opened the box and with a quizzical look on her face unfolded a camouflage uniform, a label stitched across the top left front pocket that said, SARGE. In the bottom of the box was a camouflage floppy brimmed hat with a chin strap.

Knowing some of my mother's bio, and her father's, she was a chip off that old block.

One story she told to me was corroborated by the one sister still at home at the time. An argument ensued between Josie, age seven, and her father. The details of the hiatus are lost, but Blanche described the engagement as, "fierce and fiery. Your mother said she was leaving home and ran out the back slamming the screen door behind her. But not before leaving a note." Those two versions of the event are in sync. What follows is not. The note, according to my Aunt Blanche said, "I peed in the well." My mother said she scrawled on the note with a red crayon, "I poured milk in the well."

Regardless of the version, the note created a problem, a big problem at the Ferguson house on Marshall Hill. Jake Ferguson spent the entire night, one bucket after another, attempting to sanitize the well. Meanwhile, Josie was huddled in a brake in a swale down from the house observing the entire affair and probably relishing the lie she told (*Serves him right*). Because, according to her, all was much ado about nothing. She did nothing to the well, she confessed, and the note was a ruse of revenge. Past midnight and into early morning—she had stayed there most of the night—she was driven inside by mosquitoes and had to be treated the next day for poison ivy. Taking one look at her, Jake, according to Blanche, did nothing. "She got what she deserved," was all he uttered and tried to farm the next day after a sleepless night.

On occasions, Josie was an admiral or a general, but the best and most accurate description of her was *Sarge*. If she laid down rules or made up her mind on something, whether you liked it or not, those rules would be followed.

From the time my brother and I arose in the morning until we went to bed at night, our mother had a drill for us to follow. That drill, or procedures, would change over the years, but the template remained. Perhaps, this stemmed from her father and his rigid Scottish discipline. Regardless, the drill was ever present and included the following: getting up on time, making up beds, brushing teeth (three times a day), alternating days washing dinner dishes, gathering clothes to be washed, homework always in the afternoon before listening to the radio or watching television. Though unpleasant and inconvenient at the time, from a psychologist's perspective, and both of her sons became psychologists, this structured discipline was effective parenting.

Case in point: One morning Miss Mattie Thompson, our elementary school principal, called my brother and me into the hall. She said, "Boys, your mama called." Alarms went off. Had something happened to her? Were we in trouble? She continued. "You need to go home and make up your beds." Cleveland Street Elementary School was three blocks up the street from our house. That morning, it was a *long* three blocks. From that day, into college and marriage, I have always made up my bed first thing each morning.

My mother decreed that we take Expression, also called "Speech," or "Elocution." Mrs. Imogene King was the Expression instructor. I was in the first grade. I had to memorize poems, then stand on the stage in the Cleveland Street Elementary School auditorium and recite them before a large crowd of students and parents.

Piano was next. My brother and I were to take piano lessons. We had no choice in the matter. Our mother had been taught when she was a child by Ruby her older sister. There was a piano in our home. We should learn to play it. Kicking and screaming, we were dragged into the world of music and piano lessons.

Our first piano lessons were in a small room adjacent to the auditorium at Cleveland Street Elementary School. After transferring to the junior high school across town, I began taking lessons from Mrs. R. L. ("Laura") Bouton in a house located beside First Methodist Church that also served as a temporary county library. That space is now a parking lot for the church.

Years after my mother died, while looking through my Baby Book, a slip of folded paper fell out. It was the printed program of my first piano recital under Mrs. Bouton's tutelage.

The Music Department
of
New Albany City Schools
Presents
The Pupils of Mrs. R. L. Bouton
in
A Piano Recital
High School Auditorium
May 1, 1953
Seven thirty o'clock

I played "Pirates Bold." I do not remember the piece, but I do remember being proud to finish it and exiting the stage without collapsing. Looking over the list of other performers, I was in prestigious company: Carolyn Pitner, Annice Ray Jernigan, Nancy Houston, Edith Ann Stephens, Nan Rutledge, Beverly McGaughey, Jo Kathryn Winders, Rose Clayton, Jean

Hale, and Nettie Lee Wilson, to name a few.

We have a grand piano in our home. On a regular basis, I still practice. Playing the piano or any musical instrument is a spiritual exercise. I am indebted to Mother Sarge for making the piano become an important part of my life.

One day, Sarge informed my brother and me that we were going to join the Boy Scouts. Our friends had joined, and it was time for us to join. Lester F. Sumners, a new young attorney in town, was our scoutmaster. Being in Boy Scouts meant another set of directives and laws, steps to climb: Tenderfoot, Star, Life, Eagle. We were to become Eagle Scouts. Our friends were moving in that direction, and Josie's sons would not to be outdone.

In all fairness to her, becoming an Eagle Scout would be accomplished on our own we were told. She was not going to bail us out or do the work for us. However, when we slacked off, she pushed. She motivated and encouraged. She did none of the work for us as we moved through the ranks, but she was a good shepherd. She provided guidance and kept the fire burning. Appropriately, the mother of every Scout who attains the rank of Eagle receives an Eagle pin. Josie wore two, and proudly.

One story provides an example of her leadership.

I lacked one merit badge to qualify for Eagle Scout: Fishing. One of the requirements involved catching a fish on an artificial lure. I had been fishing often with my father, an expert fisherman. But I had never caught a fish with a lure. My mom didn't do it for me, but she came up with a plan. The story is too long to tell, but she arranged for me to meet with the owner of the Phyfer place, and under his guidance, in one of the lakes on his property, *Voila*!

After my brother and I became Eagle scouts, we were inducted into the honorary Order of the Arrow. Behind the scenes of those achievements was Mother Sarge, providing guidance, encouragement, and affirmation.

The Sarge side of my mother was not limited to my brother and me.

Jimmie Rogers reflects on a colossal mistake she made while working for my mother in the jewelry store and the reprimand she received from Josie: "Don't ever empty an ashtray in the wastebasket in this store or anywhere else." The reason, of course, fire prevention.

My mother was paranoid about storms, especially tornadoes. In those days, there was no Weather Channel or emergency warning systems. We did have the weatherman reporting from Chanel 5 in Memphis at 5:00 and 10:00 each evening. If you wanted to get a heads up on the weather before waiting for the news, on radio or television, you had to improvise.

My mother may have owned the first barometer in New Albany. It still hangs in a prominent place on the wall of our old home on Cleveland Street. Besides her many talents, Josie also brushed up on meteorology. She learned how to read the barometer and instructed my father how to set up wind sensors and rain gauges in the backyard.

She told friends about her barometer. They told others. When dark clouds approached New Albany, our phone rang.

Regardless of how the sky looked, when the barometer dropped, my brother and I were told to grab our feather pillows (lightening wouldn't strike you if you were sitting on a feather pillow), and we headed for the storm cellar. The first cellar I recall was at Estelle Lamar's, which meant crossing the Tallahatchie River and driving up Moss Hill. My mother decided that was a bridge too far: we could get killed before we got there. The next protected place was in the basement of City Hall. We went there a few times the barometer dropped. The city jail was in the City Hall basement. We encountered mostly drunks, who were still drunk. That ended when my mother saw someone she knew, one of her customers. Bad for business. There were other storm shelters. They were always dank and dreary, vermin infested, the floors wet.

There seemed no situation my mother could not control. The year following our epic sojourn out west, she planned another journey, this time due north: Chicago and the Market. We stayed at the mammoth Conrad Hilton Hotel across the street from Grant Park.

We had checked into the hotel and were told we had to park the car in the hotel's garage. Dad was behind the wheel. Traffic was heavy, bumper-to-bumper. We sat for a long time in the hot car, windows down, only a slight breeze blowing from Lake Michigan. There were traffic cops, but they weren't stopping traffic long enough for my dad to back out. We sat. Mother jumped out of the car.

"Joan, what are you doing?" my dad asked.

She didn't respond.

My brother and I turned around in the back seat and watched our mother raise one hand. Traffic stopped. She motioned to dad. He followed orders and backed out. She dropped her "stop" hand and jumped into the passenger side. Policemen from three corners were blowing whistles at her. I was thankful she didn't have one.

"Joan, that could get us arrested," my dad said.

"What?" She asked.

"Impersonating a policeman."

"I was not impersonating anyone. I was just being myself," she remarked in a flair of arrogance.

My dad chuckled and said nothing.

One of the policemen stopped us and leaned his head into the car: "Ma'am, what you just did is against the law."

That famous Ferguson chin jutted out, reaching its destination before the rest of her. "Well, if you'd been doing your job, I wouldn't have had to."

Dad apologized for her. The policeman grinned and waved him on.

But mother was not through: She waved at one policeman and then the other two, a haughty Tallulah Bankhead flip of her hand as if to say, "I got you last."

Having led U. S. forces to a victory in the Pacific in World War II and having orchestrated the unconditional surrender of Japan, General Douglas A. MacArthur was leading a successful campaign against the Chinese and North Koreans on the Korean Peninsula. Then he crossed a line he had been ordered not to cross: the Yalu River bordering China. "Rank insubordination," Truman called it, and on April 11, 1951, fired MacArthur. Public outcry was over-whelming. Some called for Truman's impeachment. Gallup Poll numbers favored MacArthur 69 to 29 percent.

I remember that morning. My brother and I were eating breakfast in our kitchen. We had just finished our morning devotion. Mother was listening to the radio on the counter. The news of MacArthur's firing was reported. I had never seen her so upset. Immediately, she grabbed the phone. In those days, making a call required going through Central, the operator. She called the mayor. She called Senator John Stennis' office. She called Senator James Eastland. She called Governor Fielding Wright. "Something's got to be done," she said. "We can't lose General MacArthur."

My dad, who was from Missouri, Truman's state, was not upset. "Calm down, Joan. It's going to be okay. Truman's one of the best presidents we've ever had."

She didn't calm down. She was on a tear. She stayed on the phone most of the day, calling friends, telling them to make phone calls. She was Sarge in full charge. One of her favorite phrases was "Damn the torpedoes, full steam ahead." Once she uttered the quote and my dad murmured, "Well, full steam."

In the fourth grade, I was being bullied by one of my classmates. I came home and told my mother what he did to me. Besides breaking my glasses, he punched me in the nose. "You're going to march right back up there and tell Miss Jewel." Miss Jewel Thompson was my second-grade teacher.

I refused.

"You're going, and I'm going with you." My mother had a problem letting us, and others, fight their own fights. She had to be in the line of battle, in the thick of it. She had to be Sarge.

The next day, she accompanied me to the school. The other boy, the bully, was brought into the room with my mother, me, and Miss Jewell. But that evening, my mother received a phone call from the boy's mother. What my mother said to the lady I cannot repeat. That bully never bullied me again.

This was not the last time my mother would intervene and fight my fights for me. Picking up cues from my father, I learned to fight them myself.

When Mother Sarge didn't get her way, she manipulated. At times, it worked. At others, it didn't. The episode will be forever remembered as the "The Clingman's Dome Incident."

Our family had been to Lake Junaluska, one of our favorite places. We were headed home. Dad had decided to drive through Maggie Valley and go over the mountain to Gatlinburg. My mother was okay with his plan until we saw the sign that said "Clingman's Dome." My brother and I wanted to go. Dad wanted to go. Our mother did not like heights and protested.

My father's usual position was, "If Mama's not happy, no one is." Peace at any price. But he had his limits. As I recall the occasion, my mother was in the backseat with David, and I was up front with Dad. Dad said, "Majority rules."

Mom became frantic. She retrieved her purse from the floor and pulled out a small vial. "I'll have to take one of my pills," she exclaimed hysterically. Dad stopped the car, turned around, gave her a hard look, and said, "Take two of them because we're going." *Do you think you can handle her?* I wanted to reach over and pat my dad on the shoulder then decided, with my mom sitting directly behind me, that was one time I needed to do, and say, nothing.

On some Sundays, mother sang in the choir. Before church, I'd ask if she was going to sing. If she said, "No," I'd slip down the balcony stairs, exit the front door and run down the street to Ivy Lee Bratton's service station a block away and gather with other friends who had skipped.

Mama Sarge, however, was no dummy.

One Sunday on the way to church, she said to my father, almost too loudly, "Bill, I'm not feeling well today. I'm not singing in the choir." My father gave a conspiratorial nod. My mother and father always sat downstairs on the next to last pew. To ensure she was not in the choir, I could glance through the windows of the doors leading into the sanctuary.

I remember it was fall, football temps in the air. After the invocation, I stepped down the stairs from my perch in the balcony, glanced through the windows, and there she was, sitting beside my dad. I was out the door and headed to join my friends at Ivy Lee's. We were sitting on coke cartons talking about the Saturday football games, Ole Miss and Mississippi State, when I looked up and saw my mother. She was striding down Bankhead in the middle of the street like some gunslinger in the movies. She marched right up to me. "Get back in church, NOW!" she ordered and then turned her fiery eyes on Jay and Dan Phyfer and Herbert Graham Rogers—to name a few—and said, "And, I suggest all of you march yourselves up that hill and into church before I mention this to your parents."

Jackson Hole, Wyoming. We were on that epic "westward ho" trip. It was Sunday. Dad had left our motel room to find a newspaper. He was gone a long time and returned exasperated and angry, and without a paper. He said the paper rack he found was in front of a saloon and he was confronted by three cowboys who wanted to fight him.

"The saloon was open?" my mother questioned astonished.

"No. They were sitting on the porch."

I had seen the movie Shane the year before, and my mind conjured up images of Alan Ladd going to the general store, confronting the evil Jack Palance and his outlaw sidekick desperadoes, all sitting on the porch.

"Were there newspapers?" she pressed further.

"Yes. The stand was between where the men were sitting. I wasn't going to get into a fight in a strange place over a newspaper."

My peace-loving father. Mom began jerking, yanking on her clothes. A gunslinger slapping on his pistols came to mind.

"Joan, where are you going?"

"To get a paper."

Before he could stop her, she was out the door. I noticed she was wearing her house slippers. In ten minutes, she was back, with a newspaper.

"What did you say to them?" Dad asked.

"Not in front of the boys," she said.

Some years later, when she was visiting me in Colorado, I asked about that Sunday morning in Jackson Hole, Wyoming, a place in that time that would have been a good movie set for the gunfight at the O. K. Corral. She told me she had grabbed her movie camera on her way out of the motel room and described how she approached the three men, stopped in front of them, captured them on film, put her coin in the paper rack, lifted her paper and left.

"But what did you say to them?" I asked.

"I can't tell you."

"But I'm your grown son."

"I can't tell you."

"Forget I'm a minister. Tell me."

She shook her head.

My wife, Sandi, experienced the "Sarge" side of Josie.

She was taking her to Birmingham for a doctor's visit. I don't recall the details. All I was told of that trip, the most memorable part, was that an 18-wheeler truck driver was being difficult, and Sandi was having trouble passing him. Eventually, she did and always laughs telling how Josie flipped a wingless bird to the driver and he tooted his horn in response.

My mama Sarge.

But she was not always Sarge.

Chapter 15: Sarge with a Heart

Sarge had another side. To describe my mother as dominant, persistent, single-minded, militaristic and, at times overpowering, would omit larger, key aspects of her character, her personality, and her life. Much more than Sarge, she was loving, caring, nurturing, forgiving and merciful. She had a huge heart, one overshadowed by only one other—my father's.

You did not have to be one of her kind, of her race and religion. You did not have to side with her or agree with her. When she saw someone in need, she tried to meet that need. To someone in pain, she extended a calming, soothing hand. If she saw someone lonely, she drew them in and welcomed them. Someone naked, she clothed them. Someone with a broken heart, she embraced them and prayed with them. When she heard of a death in her community, she was one of the first knocking on the door of the residence with a casserole to feed the mourners and offer prayers to comfort. These are the behaviors observed and witnessed by the two pastors closest to her in her last hours—Reverends Leslie Nabors and Giles Lindley—that motivated and led them to call her a "saint" in their last prayers over her.

I had never seen my mother as a saint and, at first, had a negative reaction to that use of the word applied to her. But, over time, as the distance increased between the time of her death and the present, I began to realize: the saintly part of Sarge was larger than Sarge.

I recall something Anne Morrow Lindberg said about her husband Charles' death. She compared it to the felling of a mighty tree. As time moved on, she began to see the fuller depth and breadth of the man. That same metaphor applies to my experience of my mother. Following her death, I gained a depth and breadth of my mother. Not the grand dame of, at times, hyperbolic behavior, and drama. But a different, caring Sarge.

Sarge Josie could drive a hard bargain, give orders, direct traffic in Chicago and threaten to take on desperadoes on a Sunday morning in Jackson Hole, Wyoming. But the same fearless energy of that same personality also empowered a nurturing side of her.

I experienced firsthand how she helped her sister, May, care for their aging mother until she died at age 105. Mom visited her mother daily, fed her, changed her clothes and diapers, bathed her, all with a gentleness and loving spirit ... a saintly quality.

My grandmother was taken from her home and placed in a nursing home that had previously been the old Boswell's New Albany Hospital. On three occasions, my grandmother escaped from that facility. On her own, she called a taxi and directed the driver, whom I think was Flossy who drove a taxi for Ivy Lee Bratton.

That first time, my mother drove out to the old place, coaxed her mother from the front porch where she was sitting in one of the rockers and returned her to the nursing home. The second time, Mother said she was the only one at the store and instructed me to, "Go and get your grandmother. She's escaped again." With great reluctance, all of my excuses failing, I drove out to the old home place. There she was on the front porch, rocking, a beatific smile on her face. We sat together a while, rocking, and talking.

Then I said, "Grandmama, it's time to go." She pushed

herself up, reached out for my arm and allowed me to assist her down the stairs and into the car without a word spoken. It was as though all she needed to do was sit again on her porch and rock and remember, and then she was ready to go back to the nursing home.

Six months later, I remember it was summer and I was at home when Mother called. My grandmother had done it again, and I was to go get her. I refused and recall saying, "I will go out there, but not to bring her back." I don't know what my mother did because I hung up.

The next day I went to see my grandmother at the nursing home on the hill across from the Courthouse. She was sitting on the porch that faced the Courthouse, rocking, that same beatific grin, or smirk, on her face, as if she'd stolen a cookie from the cookie jar and gotten away with it. Or convinced herself she had.

Years after her mother died on August 25, 1978, Josie extended the same patient care for her sister, May. The other siblings lived away, except Ruby on Cleveland Street and Robbie in Memphis, but they had their own issues. The responsibilities for taking care of May fell on my mother's shoulders.

On another occasion, Josie rushed to Michigan City to care for her niece Lucy, Blanche's daughter. Lucy had been thrown from a horse and severely injured.

In my mother's last days, when my brother and I could not spend the night with her in the hospital in New Albany, Lucy drove from Oxford, left her responsibilities as house mother of the Sigma Chi fraternity at Ole Miss and stayed with her. And it was Lucy who came immediately to console us after she died.

***

His name was LC. No period after L and C. Just LC. He was slender, nice-looking, well-mannered.

From nowhere it seemed, one day LC appeared on my mother's doorstep and knocked on the front door. The story, as she related it, was filled with caution. She did not know, had never seen, the young, slender, nice-looking black man, a teenager at the time, standing before her. But he knew her name, called her Miss Joan and said he was LC, no last name provided. He wanted to rake her leaves. She asked how he knew her name and her address. According to her, he said, "My Granddaddy told me."

"Your Granddaddy?"

"Yessum. My Granddaddy Giles."

My mother said she let out a shriek that "scared him to death," grabbed him in a hug and pulled him through the door into the house.

"How old are you?" she enquired.

"Fifteen."

"But your Granddaddy's been dead a while," she recalled responding. "How could he tell you about me?"

"Actually, he told my mama before he died that if ever any of his family needed anything that Miss Joan Morris would help them." He went on to inform her that most of his granddaddy's children were still alive and working. He told her that his mother worked for a white lady across town, someone my mother knew and saw on a frequent basis, socially and in business.

Other questions followed. What did LC stand for? He answered, "My parents had so many kids they just run out of names and called me LC." What was he going to do with the money my mother was going to pay him because she knew she was going to hire him? What were his goals in life? He told her he was earning the money to save up so he could go to college.

Long, long story short, my mother took LC under her wing, followed him through high school, paid most of his tuition to enter a community college and later a four-year college where he graduated with honors. There were many other things she did for LC. At her funeral, I realized the full impact of that saintly side of her upon another person, one of a different color. LC sat on the front pew with family and openly wept, at times sobbed, throughout the entire service, and again at her graveside.

As I was writing this last segment, I called my brother: "Whatever happened to LC?" David said he was able to get him a job with the Mississippi School for the Blind and Deaf. "He had to take courses in sign language at Mississippi State which I paid for. He worked at the school and retired a few years ago."

I could continue about the help Josie provided for others, but this one story stands out. Using the tree metaphor again, my different perception of my mother actually began after another tree fell: my father. On that same visit to Colorado Springs to visit me following his death, she assembled a picnic basket and we drove up Ute Pass, sat on the rocks beside a brook and she began to talk. What she unloaded on me was stunning, things about my dad I never knew.

Earlier in this narrative, I spoke of my father's previous marriage, the problems in that relationship. Meredith's battle with drugs and alcohol. Her placement in a sanitarium. The subsequent divorce and collapse of my father's business. I knew none of that history until this special time with Mom after his death. I also learned from her that my father took care of Meredith. He visited her when he was in Corinth and in New Albany, sent money, care packages, often driving to the sanitarium and visiting her. Before they married, my father asked my mother to promise him two things. One was embedded in their marriage vows. The other was, if something happened to him, for Josie to continue caring for Meredith.

Josie kept that promise.

I did not know when Meredith died. After I graduated from seminary in 1969, I was rarely home. I was pastoring churches or above the Arctic Circle serving as a chaplain on the Distant Early Warning Line (DEWLine). Only recently, going through the layers of papers, letters, and invoices, I found a small envelope, the size in which one would send a thank you or sympathy note. It was dated June 6, 1980, ten years after my father's death on June 7, 1970. With delicate care, I loosened the flap with a letter opener, removed the card inside, read the short note. The superintendent of the sanitarium in Tennessee had sent my mother a note informing her of Meredith Morris' death, stating her belongings would be shipped later.

If ever there was an angel of mercy on this earth, it was my mother. When those two pastors, on her deathbed, called her a saint, they got it right.

Saint Sarge.

Has a nice ring to it.

Figure 26 Josie, David, Olivia, Daniel, Rosemarie, and Aunt Blanche

Figure 27 Christmas at Josie's circa. 1992 JE, Meredith, Jason, Jonathan, Daniel, Olivia (back row); Sandi, Anna Katherine, Josie (seated)

Chapter 16: The Long Arm of Josie

Based upon the following events, you might conclude Josie was a "control freak." Or you might decide she possessed a template of parenting passed down to her over the ages. Then again, you may opine she had a sixth sense when it came to her elder son or a combination of the above with a dose of divine omniscience. Other options may cross your mind.

The first experiences of my mother's keen, omniscient sense of detecting my whereabouts came when I was a child playing in our neighborhood. I had created hiding places on the block and beyond. Hiding places no one knew, not even my closest friends. They were secret places where I could go and just "be." At times, dream. Or cook up fantasies to be lived in real time, real life—Superman, Captain Marvel, Batman, Robin, Tarzan, Bomba the Jungle Boy. And, there were times I went to these arcane dens to escape my mother's wrath.

No one ever found my private places.

No one.

Except, my mom.

Usually, I'd get an advance notice, her shrill whistle signaling me to come home. Or her heavy footsteps. Then she'd pull back a matted grass curtain, or open a cellar door, or shake a tree.

That was just the beginning, a foreshadowing of later acts of clairvoyance. The occasions are multiple. A few are noteworthy.

As budding Boy Scouts, some of our Troop 18 had decided to go on a survival trip, also known, and remembered, as *The*

Five Mile Hike. Joe Tyson Wilkins, III, a.k.a., Jo Jo, wrote this story:

One of the requirements for 1st Class scout is the 5-mile hike. We, Joe Edd, Bill Rutledge, maybe Phil Morris and I planned for this Saturday excursion by having my dad, JT Wilkins, locate a safe meandering gravel road on which we could march and take breaks, especially for lunch during which time we would cook our meal and thereby complete the 1st class requirements for cooking. Not a three-course meal by any stretch of the imagination.

The hike began west of Myrtle and curved around south returning into Hwy 78 where we would be picked up. The distance was right at 5 miles with no hills, light traffic, wooded areas along the road and perfect places for us to prepare our gourmet lunch using Boy Scout training and ancient Indian lore, but with matches.

We carried our water in canteens and food and cooking utensils in our backpacks. About noon, we all were ready to break for lunch and cook our food. We gathered firewood, started our cooking fires, and got our skillets ready, all except Joe Edd. He must have planned only for the hike, as he had no food for lunch—not a can of soup, not an apple, not a piece of bread. Thinking back, I do not recall anyone being sympathetic to Joe Edd and not a crumb was offered to the suffering, woebegone Scout.

We had watched each other carefully on the hike. None of us knew where we were and did not think that any parent could possibly find us in this remote area of the county. That era had no cell phones or other means of communication should we need to contact our parents. But wait, as we were firing up our meals and as Joe Edd sat there with his forlorn look, we hear in the distance a car moving down the road and the horn blasting. A big maroon Buick winds down the road. It is Joan delivering Joe Edd's meal to him. What could it be? It was wrapped in grocery store paper, white with tape binding it. It had to be from Daniel's Grocery meat counter. Sure enough, it was a big juicy steak. We all gathered around to look at it and compare it to our hamburger steak, minute steak, snf baloney we had to eat. By this time, we had finished our meal and sat to watch Joe Edd cook and devour his steak.

The story of my mother's omniscience related to that particular time stops here, but the rest was too delicious for Jo Jo to omit.

Joe Edd nonchalantly pulled his black skillet from his knapsack and promptly placed it on the blazing fire with his big steak and it began to sizzle, immediately. We sat back to observe this display of culinary expertise as he moved onward to his gourmet meal. He was enjoying the moment, casting a glance and wry smile at all of us. Things went well initially, and the smell and sizzle were a treat for all. But then, smoke appeared, and flames jumped from the skillet. The intense heat had caught the grease on fire. We jumped back with only Joe Edd in attendance, and he grabbed a cap to hold in his hand and picked up the skillet handle. What to do with a grease fire in the wilderness?

Joe Edd's training as a 2nd class Scout emerged and took immediate action to control the situation and to not endanger any of us nor the environment. He dispatched the steak in the air at least twenty feet and back over his head. It was too high and too far for him to catch it in the air as Aunt Jemima might do with pancakes and it landed in a nice, clear sandy area.

We were stunned, speechless, and for a long time, no one said a word as we focused on the gritty steak. Could it be saved? We turned to Joe Edd with his forlorn look and long face. His stomach growled loudly, but we pretended not to hear.

There was no water to spare to clean the steak and time was slipping away. Joe Edd made it on raisins, a piece of bread, some nabs, etc. Joe Edd did pass his cooking requirements for 1st class and went on to get his cooking Merit Badge. That withstanding, someone else did the cooking when Joe Edd was about.

I often wake up at night wondering what happened to that steak. Our lips were sealed when we returned to New Albany and the rest of the Scout Troop—Yes, we had a great time. Joan never knew the full story, and our lips have remained sealed until this very day. Further, I saith not.

One evening in my teens, there was a party across town at Ann Ray's new house on Glade Street. I did not yet have my driver's license, so I must have been fifteen. You could have a permit at age 15, but I was not allowed to have one until I was 16. I recalled being picked up by Jo Jo who did have his license.

The party started early, around six o'clock. I was told by my mother to be home by nine. Her time frames were non-negotiable. Nine o'clock meant NINE O'CLOCK! Near nine o'clock, I told Jo Jo I had to go home. He was not ready to leave, nor was I. But I felt my mama's long arm flexing, stretching, reaching.

I left the party and began walking home. My house was across town, a distant walk in those days. But I thought I knew the way. For some reason, I turned right at the next block where I should have gone straight. Within a few minutes, I realized I was in the "colored" part of town that was called "The Dum."

Most people had another pejorative name for it, but my parents called it The Dum. My mother said she didn't know why it was called The Dum but said it had nothing to do with race or intelligence and spelled it for me: D-U-M. She said if I didn't like that word, we could call it The Quarters. That was better. But for some reason, perhaps because it was so unusual and signified absolutely nothing, Dum still hung in my mind.

Walking home that night through the Dum in the dark, the tune from a popular television detective show, *Dragnet*, played in my mind over and over: "Dum, ta, dum, dum." I passed groups of friendly blacks who spoke kindly and waved. There were no cell phones in those days. No way of communicating except by house phones, and I was too frightened to knock on a door or ask for help in The Dum.

I tried to turn around and back track to Glade but took another wrong turn and headed deeper into The Dum ... dum ta dum dum. And deeper into trouble ... dum ta dum dum ... I was on a narrow street, a few houses either side, when I stumbled, literally, into a cemetery. If it were the cemetery, I thought it was, I had a vague idea of my location. Highway 78 ran through the city cemetery. If I kept going straight and crossed the highway, I'd run into the Frisco railroad tracks where I could take a left turn and follow the tracks to the shirt factory on Highland Street. Cleveland was one street over.

But I never got the chance to prove my Scout lore finding my way home. Before I could reach the highway, car lights suddenly bounced into the cemetery and headed straight toward me. Frightened, I jumped behind a large tombstone.

The lights stopped. Someone I couldn't see, because of the glare, got out of the car. Then a familiar woman's voice. "Edd? Joe Edd?"

I dreaded what would happen next. But my mother, with hugs and kisses, was glad to see me. "My God! My God!" she exclaimed. "I thought you might have been dead." I've always wondered if that was why her thoughts led her to the cemetery. The long arm of Sarge, stretching even into the city of the dead. I had learned not to ask her how she found me. She just always did.

I was never punished for that episode, and she never changed. Curfews were curfews. Sarge was Sarge.

Within that same time frame, another situation developed. I was in the eleventh grade. Hall Junior Wilbanks called and asked if I would like to go on a coon hunt with him and John David Pennebaker. My mother gave her okay, my dad agreed, and I embarked on what came to be known, and always remembered, as *THE Coon Hunt*.

Hall Junior picked me up around 9:30 on a Saturday evening. My mom asked Hall Junior where we were coon hunting, and all I recall he said was, "In the county out east." He told her he would have me home about midnight. John

David, who lived two houses behind ours, was picked up next.

The time was around ten o'clock p.m. when the three of us entered the woods around Blue Springs in east Union County. At first, all went well. The dogs treed a coon. But their barking was a long way from where we were sitting on a log. We started running. I was running blind because Hall Junior was the only one with a flashlight, John David was behind him. Those were the days when John David was, let's say, corpulent. I heard a splash, then a second splash. The next thing I knew I was in a creek atop John David's shoulders. The dogs were still barking. Eventually, we found the tree and the dogs and the coon. But we had no idea where we were. The time was past midnight when I was supposed to be home. We spent most of the night thrashing through woods hoping to emerge on a road or find a house, anything that would orient us.

At daybreak, we stumbled onto a gravel road. Exhausted, we flung ourselves down on a grassy knoll beside the road and rested. And thought, Hall Junior thinking longer about where he'd parked his truck. We'd been lying in the grass for about half an hour, still thinking, wondering and the sound of a motor pierced our ears. Not a car or truck motor. We looked up and a plane was circling overhead. I will never forget the immediate words from John David's mouth: "Joe Edd, your mama's got the air patrol looking for us." Everyone laughed.

John David's comment was close. My mother had called the Sheriff's Department and had had them issue an all-points bulletin. We waved our arms wildly, and soon, a sheriff's patrol car arrived. Hall Junior's pickup was a few miles away, near Highway 78. We thought we had lost the three dogs, but they were huddled around the pickup.

My mom and dad were not angry, just thrilled we were

alive. But I was ordered to clean up and go to church.

As I grew older, I thought my mother's obsessive need to always know my whereabouts would diminish. Hopefully, disappear completely. At least wear itself out. But it only became more refined, and piercingly laser accurate.

The year was 1964. I was attending Millsaps College and headed home a day early for Christmas break. When I got to Batesville, an idea bloomed. I had not seen or heard from an ex-girlfriend in several months. We had remained on good terms. I knew she was in Memphis attending nursing school. I had a phone number. I hooked a left onto Highway 61 and headed north.

I arrived in Memphis at the Admiral Benbow Inn around seven o'clock. Carol and her roommate were glad to see me. They were staying at the Admiral Benbow, across the street from Methodist Hospital, until their apartment was ready. We had a round of drinks, ordered a pizza and were enjoying reliving better days and the phone rang. Carol picked up the receiver, and I watched her face screw up.

"Yes! Yes! He's right here," she said and handed me the phone.

I cringed. Only one person had the ability to find me regardless of time, place and/or circumstance.

"What are you doing there?" my mother's stern voice questioned.

No signs of weakening or dying, the clairvoyance only got stronger. The long arm longer.

The next year, I graduated from Millsaps College and had

been accepted at the University of Edinburgh in Scotland for my first year of seminary. I had accomplished the transition proudly on my own, including obtaining a pastorate at the oldest Methodist church in Scotland at Dunbar, about thirty miles from Edinburgh. The church was founded by John and Charles Wesley.

A chip off the old traveling block, I had also made all the travel arrangements by myself. First to Washington D.C. by train, where I stayed a few days with one of Mother's best friends, M. J. Black, and her family. The next leg was a long train trip through New York City, changing trains from Penn Station to Grand Central Station for the last train journey through New Hampshire to Montreal, Canada. In Montreal, I was to board *The Carinthian*, an ocean cruiser of the Cunard Line, for a seven-day trans-Atlantic voyage to Greenock, Scotland, near Glasgow, where the Titanic was built. I had shipped ahead two large trunks and had to pick them up at sheds 2 and 3 at the foot of Saint Francois Xavier Street the day before the ship sailed on September 3, 1965.

The trip, all the way from Middleton, Tennessee, where I caught the train to D.C., the transfers in New York City and arrival in Montreal went off without a hitch. I had thought. In my "careful" planning, I'd forgotten to secure lodging in Montreal. I am standing outside the Montreal train station with my luggage and nowhere to go. I hailed a taxi, and the driver was very helpful. He said there were five large hotels in Montreal. He recommended The Laurentian.

He deposited me at the door of the hotel and waited for me to ensure I could get a room. One was available. I gave him a thumbs up and a generous tip. As I settled into my room, I thought, *I need to call home and let Mom and Dad know I had arrived safely along with my location.* I picked up the phone to dial the hotel operator. A familiar voice blew through the receiver: "Edd! Edd!" (Looking back, when my mother called my name, it was usually never with a question.) "How in the world?" I said.

She told me she had obtained the names and phone numbers of the largest hotels in Montreal and commenced calling. "On the fifth, The Laurentian, they put me through to your room."

Scary. Was there any place in the world I could go, and my mother could not find me? I thought of Psalm 139. Did she have a direct line? Was there any place beyond her incredible reach?

Then, there was my bother David's wedding in Switzerland in 1970. I was serving a church in Colorado Springs and decided to attend the ceremony. The wedding took place in a 12th century church overlooking Lake Neuchatel. Mother was present with a retinue of friends that included Lilly Francis McGill, her daughter, Margaret, and son, James. Roger McMillen was David's best man. The dinner and dance by the lake after the wedding were memorable.

After the wedding, I met Mother, Lilly Francis, her children and Roger and his brother, Leroy, in Florence, Italy. After a few days of fun in that price-less city, I took off by train for Nice on the Riviera. After enjoying Nice for a week, I traveled to see my Aunt Blanche in Madrid. The train ride was the longest of my life and included almost being thrown into jail in Barcelona by a Guardia Civil because I entered the station through the wrong door.

Upon my arrival in Madrid, Aunt Blanche showed me

around. I became deathly ill because of anchovies I had eaten at a midnight kiosk in Barcelona. She finally put me on a plane to London. In the back of my mind, I had a vague notion my mother was in London with Lilly Francis, Margaret, and James, but I did not know for sure. I did have the name of a hotel where she might be staying, all of these thoughts only supposition and speculation.

After arriving at Heathrow in London and collecting my valise, I took one of London's famous black taxis into the city where I took a Tube to Kensington Square. I climbed the stairs from the subway onto the street, took a few steps into the night air, and heard *that* voice. "Edd! Joe Edd! Over here!"

Across on the opposite street corner stood my mother, waving wildly. I was glad to see her. She said she had had been in contact with Aunt Blanche who told her I was arriving by plane. The only other information Mom had was the name of the hotel she had given to me before I had left Florence.

All I could think was, *"She's god."* And thought again of Psalm 139.

Figure 28. Josie and Bill Blizzard at Meredith and Joey's wedding

Chapter 17: The Second Bill

I do not know the year, or the season, much less the date. But sometime in 1995, Josie heard a light rap at the front door of her home on Cleveland Street. She thought nothing of it, and then heard it again. She said, as she told the story, that she was in the kitchen, still in her housecoat, placing the time of day around noon, or later. She opened the door and said she saw this nicely dressed handsome man standing there and did not, at first, recognize him until he said, "Joan, it's been a long time."

"Bill Blizzard!" she squealed.

When my father died in 1970, my mother was fifty-two years old and still an attractive, youthful lady with ageless dynamite legs that flirted with each other when she sashayed. She continued wearing her wedding band. She told me, my brother and closest friends that she would never remarry: "Bill is still with me. I can feel him. I talk to him. He helps me make decisions." That was that. None of us gave the possibility of her remarrying any further thought.

She kept the store running with some success and started her own antique business on the side. That was not all. I've mentioned her multi-purpose business card. She had her fingers in several pies. She eventually sold the store again (Morris Brothers Jewelry Store) and auctioned its contents. Her business interests winnowed to gems and antiques. With her astute business sense, she reasoned that she could buy stones and antiques and sell them from a booth in one of the antique shops in Tupelo and New Albany. She had little antique nooks here and there. She was prospering.

Her love of antiques led to a renewed fascination with flea markets. She was drawn to them. When Josie went to flea markets, she made things happen.

At First Monday in Ripley, Mississippi, about twenty miles north of New Albany, she met an old friend from days before she met Bill Morris. His name was Alec McKenzie. He was from Pascagoula, Mississippi, on the Gulf Coast. Alec was affable, sociable, and easy going, seemingly a good match with Josie. He saw himself fitting in with her cluster of friends and social network. What he did not calculate, or miscalculated, was fitting in with Josie.

My father never told me how he responded to Jake Ferguson's statement about being able to manage his daughter. I learned later, looking back, and wearing my psychologist hat, that Bill Morris managed Josie by not managing her. In short, as likable, and easy going as he appeared, Alec McKenzie was not Bill Morris. Odds were stacked against the marriage. My brother offered to pay for a month cruise so they would, "get to know each other better." The offer was declined. Despite the odds, on February 11, 1984, I married them at the chancel of First United Methodist Church, the same place where my mother and father exchanged vows on June 15, 1941.

Seven years later, on March 28, 1991, Alec had a fatal heart attack. He was in his army surplus store on Main Street in New Albany, the same store where our children conspiratorially purchased the Sarge uniform. His doctor said he was dead before he hit the concrete floor.

The days prior to Alec's burial were marked with strife. Josie had never been fully accepted by Alec's Pascagoula, Mississippi, family, and some within her family had not gracefully accepted him. Words were spoken by both sides. A lull in the conflict occurred when all parties had lunch the day of his funeral at Josie's. True to her classic form, she served up a feast. I was asked to say the blessing, weaving into a longer grace than I am accustomed to saying, strands of supplication for peace and harmony. But alas, after dessert, the cries of who got what commenced and continued for over a year. Because changing her name back to Morris was too much trouble—driver's license, legal documents, etc.—Josie retained McKenzie.

Like an oar swirl, Alec's death seemed to speed away quickly.

In 1991, Josie was an attractive seventy-three years young and vowed, after the dust had settled and the air had cleared, "I will never ever get involved with another man."

Until that knock on the door of her home on Cleveland Street that day and, "Bill Blizzard!"

My memories of Bill "Devan" Blizzard are warmly vivid. Growing up, I saw him only at a distance. His mother lived in the home where he grew up with his two sisters, across Cleveland Street from the home where I grew up, the home where he knocked on the door that morning. I saw him from time to time sitting in a rocker smoking a cigar on his mother's porch. At times, he brought his son, Billy, and daughter, Betty, and occasionally his wife, Lillian. Billy and I became close friends and always enjoyed playing together on his visits to see his grandmother.

Intermittently, I would see Mr. Blizzard ambling around New Albany, his hands folded behind his back, his head up turning left and right, taking in all the memories of the place and of his youth. Most of the time, I would see him in Rogers Rexall Drug Store which was next to my parents' jewelry store. He always sat at one of the wrought-iron marble-topped tables, his feet propped up on the table's edge, smoking a cigar and chatting with Mr. Lee Rogers, the pharmacist and owner of the store and the father of my first girlfriend, Ann. With a grand smile, Mr. Blizzard always spoke to me first and always called me by my full name, Joe Edd Morris. He was Hollywood, Tyrone Power handsome and had the look of someone who was important, though not trying to look important. In my childhood and emerging adolescence, he seemed genuinely interested in me, ensuring that impression each time he saw me with, "How are you doing, Joe Edd Morris?" or "What are you doing these days, Joe Edd Morris?"

From those halcyon days of my youth, I would not see Bill Blizzard again until 1965 when I was a student enrolled at the University of Edinburgh's New College, School of Theology. In my mother's usual fashion, she was making things happen. Before I left for Scotland, she informed me that Bill Blizzard and Lillian, his wife, were living in London, that he was "high up" with Cummins Diesel and in their London office where he was the executive manager over their Great Britain network. That information piqued my interest, but she revved it up a notch. "And they are living just one block from Buckingham Palace in a house formerly owned and purchased from Ronald Reagan and Jane Wyman."

Because I had fifty percent of my mother's genes, rubbing up against fame and prestige was in the mix. My first month in Scotland I spent hitchhiking around the scenic highlands, meeting interesting people who bought meals for me and ensured I had a place to stay each evening. The longest I had ever been away from home was a few weeks at Camp Lake Stephens in north Mississippi and on the National Boy Scout Jamboree at Valley Forge, Pennsylvania, in 1957. I grew lonesome and homesick. Mother had given me a phone number for the Blizzards in London. They were delighted to hear from me, especially Billy.

A midnight flight from Edinburgh to London cost a little more than two pounds, roughly five dollars in American money. As traveler's luck would have it, I sat by a man on the plane who lived two blocks from the Blizzards' address, which I had shown to him. He drove me to their front door. Billy was up waiting for me. I spent a grand weekend being wined and dined around London. One night, Bill drove us around the city and pointed out all of the sights. I was mesmerized, not so much with the sights, but with his interest in me and devotion to ensuring I enjoyed my visit. I had no idea this man would bring an abundance of happiness to my mother in her last years on this planet.

I visited the Blizzards several more times during my year in Edinburgh and convalesced there Christmas following a skiing incident in St. Moritz, Switzerland, a harrowing experience on the side of a mountain.

All of the above occurred in 1965-1966.

The next time I saw Bill Blizzard I was with my wife Sandi. He was sitting beside my mother in her living room on Cleveland Street. They were holding hands and smiling warmly at each other, love lights twinkling in their eyes.

Sandi and I were quickly brought up to speed.

Bill Blizzard spoke first. He said that after burying his wife Lillian, he returned to Tampa where they had a home and a beach house on the Gulf. He said that though retired, he was still active in the affairs of Cummins Diesel and that he had investment interests and worked out daily at a wellness center near his home. He enjoyed playing weekly golf and had many friends at the country club where he was a member.

Then came the "but."

"But something was missing in my life," he said looking at my mother. "I missed having a partner. My yearning turned north, to Mississippi, more specifically, to New Albany, Mississippi." He was still looking at my mother.

From his friends in New Albany, he said he had done some investigating and learned that my mother's second husband, Alec McKenzie, had died in 1991. It had been about as many years since his wife's death, which had been a slow and tortuous process. He had thought it might be timely to return to New Albany and "pay your mother a visit."

Mother was, "shocked, beyond belief," she said, to open the door and see "Bill Blizzard!"

At this point in the conversation, my mother picked up the thread. She said, with a lilt in her voice, that she invited him in, and they sat in the living room the rest of the day visiting old memories.

Somewhere in their conversation, Mother had said, "Bill, I had always looked upon you as my best friend's brother."

"But, Joan," he said, smiling, "I had never looked upon you as my sister's best friend."

I think that was the moment the fire fell. My mother was one for cutting to the chase and not wasting time. Apparently, William "Bill" Devan Blizzard was, too. *Time is for growing butter beans.*

From that point forward, until her death on September 15,

2004, Josie and Bill Blizzard invested in and brought a second round of happiness in each other's lives.

One day, Sandi and I took them out to lunch in Tupelo at Applebee's. The four of us sat at one of the tall round tables. I had dropped my napkin, and when I bent down to pick it up, I observed that my mother and Bill Blizzard were playing footsies. It was a touching, romantic moment and reminded me that love, playful love at that, has no age limit. They were like two teenagers who had just fallen for each other.

Their physical attraction for each other brings up another aspect to their relationship. Early on, Bill had told my mother about some medical, urological issues that precluded physical intimacy. She had told him that did not matter, that she had given up cigarette smoking, she could give up sex. So, the romantic flirtation I glimpsed that day at Applebee's was a reflection of *agape* love something deep and mature and ageless.

When they were together, in deference to each other's children and close friends, they maintained a proper decorum. When Mother traveled to Tampa to spend time with Bill and his children, she stayed in his beach house, but most of their time together was spent in New Albany. Both had decided that Bill could, and should, stay in the house with her and in separate bedrooms. This arrangement was made all the more appropriate and acceptable because mother's good friend, Jimmie Rogers, was renting and living upstairs at the time. Mother and Bill commented frequently that they had a chaperone. Most did not know the full story regarding Bill's medical issues, and he and my mother had decided it did not matter. They were both over seventy-five years of age and, "could do what we damn well please," said Josie on one occasion in that old Sarge voice.

In August and September of 2004, as my mother lay dying in the Union County Baptist Memorial Hospital, Bill Blizzard was by her side every day. I thought of his devotion to his wife, Lillian, how he had been at her bedside and taken care of her during her long battle with cancer. Now, he was doing the same with the second woman in his life and her battle with cancer—leukemia.

The night before my mother died, he and I sat on the front porch of her home, the same house where I grew up, across the street from the same house where he grew up, and reminisced. He spoke lovingly of my mother as a devoted companion, as someone who had indefatigable energy, a spirit of adventure and a need to continue to travel and see the world. "That was just what I needed," he said. "I could never replace Bill Morris, but I think she needed me, too." I agreed. Like my father, he had never tried to control her and that seemed to be the magic formula for a good mix and "managing" Josie.

As we sat there in that balmy September night, knowing my mother would probably not live through the night, I could see the end of the block and Peterson Avenue. I recalled the article from the *New Albany Gazette* he had saved and sent to me, the story he remembered of Aunt Rose Peterson, and the memory evoked the meaning of neighbors and friends and how across time they had intersected our lives and contributed to who we are and who we became and are becoming.

The next morning, my mother died. Bill Blizzard arrived shortly afterwards at the hospital. Her room had cleared, and I was sitting there in a corner chair. Bill was standing next to the bed beside her. He reached over and held her hand that was still warm. Suddenly, he began sobbing. I quickly left the room to allow him that private time with the love of his life, closed the door and told others not to enter. The men from the funeral home arrived to take her, and I asked them to wait. During the funeral, Bill sat with the immediate family, and from the dais where I sat, I could see him brushing back tears. Josie was eighty-six. He was eighty-five.

I loved William "Bill" Devan Blizzard and still do. I felt as close to him as if he had been my own father. Five years later, on his ninetieth birthday, I flew to Tampa for the celebration. His son Billy, my longtime Cleveland Street friend, picked me up at the hotel where I was staying and took me to the country club for the party. I wore a white dinner jacket, and when I arrived, the only other person in the room wearing a white dinner jacket was Bill Blizzard. It was a grand and memorable occasion. I flew back the next day knowing I would probably never see him again. And I did not. But his memory visits me often and profoundly. In her last years, he gave my mother some of her best days. Besides my father, the second Bill was the classiest guy I had ever known.

Figure 29. Joan and Bill Blizzard

Photos of Joan and Bill Blizzard

Chapter 18: Last Days

The first notation in my journal of any indication that my mother was having health problems was Monday, September 15, 2003: "Spoke with David about Mom - he's pessimistic—I'm upbeat." That was the entry. Nothing else related to, or was about, any medical condition. Prior to that entry, regular visits, and church attendances with her were noted. A few days before, on Friday the 12th, I had helped her in her yard, and she had given me some plants, which I took home and planted immediately. But there is nothing in the brief entry specifically about health issues. However, there was something significant, ironic, about the date of that notation. One year later, on September 15th, she died.

Slowly turning the journal page, I came to Wednesday, September 24: "Met Mom at the cancer center—Dr. Christopher C. Croot did not have good news: "Mylodysphasia, precancerous leukemia—she's holding her own now, but the prognosis is guarded too poor." I was sitting behind Mom when she received the news. I could not see her face. I saw her head and shoulders dip slightly and then snap back erect, her body characteristically straighten as she said, "Well, I've lived a good long life."

I recall being shaken and on the verge of tears, but felt I needed to hold up for her. I stood, put my arm around her and said, "Mom, I am sorry. I love you." Then we left and, in silence, I walked her to her car where I hugged her again and told her I loved her again. She stood erect, chin up, tight-lipped, her eyes steely, and with no emotion thanked me. I watched as she drove away and when she could not see me, in a parking lot I no longer remember, I broke down.

On Tuesday, October 4th, I spoke with her by phone. She said the hospital had run some tests and would be conducting bone marrow tests on Wednesday, the 5th, and then added brightly, "I like my doctors." Thursday, I called her about the bone marrow tests. She said, "They were painful, but I didn't holler." The tests eventually returned negative, which was good news.

On Thursday October 23rd, Sandi and I drove to Ocean Springs, Mississippi, for the annual Mississippi Library Association banquet for me to receive the award for Best Fiction of 2002. When I lauded my mother in that presentation, and said "Someday, Mother, I'm going to write about you and in a big way," I felt very close to her. In her declining days or years—no one knew at that time how long she had—she felt proud that she and my father had given two successful sons to the world, one a minister and writer who would bury and memorialize her.

On Sunday, September 26th, the article about my novel, *Land Where My Fathers Died*, receiving the Mississippi Library Association's Best Fiction of 2002 was in the *Northeast Daily Journal*. Sandi and I attended church with her and Bill Blizzard in New Albany. Her pride was obvious as members of my home church, her friends, lavished us both with compliments and "prouds." The rest of that day was more meaningful. After lunch at Punkin Center, a small, rural community between Myrtle and New Albany, my mom and Bill took Sandi and me on a pilgrimage back through time, touring old Highway 78 and Myrtle. The two of them intertwined tales and memories of those days, their days. In those timeless moments, none of us were thinking about what might lie ahead. All four of us were absorbing as much as we could from the strong pulse of those vibrant and happy days.

A few Sundays later, October 16, Sandi dropped me off in New Albany. She went to check on her parents in Ingomar. I attended church with Mom, and afterwards we ate again at Punkin Center. Then Mom drove me over old country roads, revisiting places of her youth. I observed and listened with fascination. Not at the sights, but this private time with my mother as I listened to her crystal-clear memories of places and people. The thought occurred to me; *I should be writing all of this down.* But I did not need to record the memory of being with her, just the two of us. No time before in my life could I recall this private one-on-one time with my mother. I felt closer to her, so affirmed and at peace. And, I knew those feelings were reciprocal.

Christmas, 2003. A keen awareness prevailed among all of us that this might be Josie's last Christmas. Sandi and I attended Christmas Eve services in New Albany with mother and Bill Blizzard. David was there with his three children—Jonathan, Olivia, and Daniel. On Christmas Day, we celebrated at Mom's house, sharing presents around the tree and food and fellowship around the long dining table. The decorations, food and ambiance were quintessential Josie. This day was a fun time devoid of any thoughts of her leukemia. She was her usual buoyant, vivacious, robust self. If anyone from outside had observed, they would not have had the slightest notion this would be the last Christmas celebrated in Josie's home on Cleveland Street.

During that holiday season, Sandi and I had been made aware of a serious medical issue, but it was not my mom's. Dr. Rud Robison, during a routine checkup, became concerned about the condition of my heart. On December 31st, tests at Cardiology revealed a valve malfunction and several blockages. Blood was also running too fast through my carotid arteries. On January 16, following a stress test and heart catherization, we received the alarming news, alarming because I had been running two miles a day. I had aorta and carotid blockages as well as narrowing of heart vessels. Bottom line: open heart surgery on January 30th, quadruple bypass, and an aortic valve replacement.

My mother did not need this news on top of her medical issues, but she was an inspiration. She had had open heart surgery, and the same physician, Dr. Max Hutchinson, would be my surgeon. I felt strong and ready for the surgery, but not ready to tell her. When I did tell her, she was with Bill Blizzard in Florida where they would be for the winter. I told her she did not need to be present for this surgery. It was the same she had had, and I would be fine. She and Bill Blizzard did not need to make a 14-hour drive from Tampa then turn around and drive back. With great, and tearful, reluctance, she accepted my request.

During the first months of 2004, my mother remained in Florida, staying in Bill Blizzard's guest beach house. Except for occasional phone calls, I had little other contact with her. She appeared to be doing fine, at least her tough mental exterior said she was *fine*.

On Mother's Day, May 9, Mom had returned home from Florida and I attended church with her and drove her and Jimmie Rogers to the Blue Mountain College cafeteria for lunch. We had a grand time. Afterwards, I brought her plants from my greenhouse I'd wintered for her and helped her in her yard. She appeared healthy and energized, her old self. I could tell no difference in her, certainly nothing consistent with a leukemia diagnosis. I thought perhaps, along with her strong and tough constitution and radiation treatments, it had gone into remission.

On Sunday, July 11, Sandi, and I attended church in New Albany with Mother and Bill Blizzard, and afterward we were luncheon guests of Joe and Joyce Parks.

Sometime after that visit, no one has been able to pinpoint the date, Mother went to Memphis with Jimmie Rogers, Lily Francis McGill and her daughters, Margaret, and Jamie Sue. It has been determined by Margaret that they attend an Andre Rieu concert. They stayed at The Orleans Hotel in Overton Square. Mother injured her leg on part of the bed frame in the room where they were staying. Jimmie says, "She cut her leg, it was awful. The next morning, we wrapped it in a towel. At checkout, your mother told the management about the incident, and they comped our room. At that point, it just looked like a nick."

On Sunday July 25th, I was back in New Albany teaching the Majorie Houston Class, Mom's Sunday school class. Sitting beside her in church, I noticed a spot on her left leg, a discoloration that resembled a bruise. I asked her about it, but she brushed it off, telling me the story of the incident at The Orleans. Three Sundays later, August 15, Sandi and I attended church with mother and Bill Blizzard. The mark was still on her leg, and it looked larger and darker. I asked her again about it, and again she disregarded it as nothing serious.

Four days later, August 19—Bill Blizzard's 85th birthday—he and Mother were to go to Joyce and Joe Park's cabin at Darden for a celebration party. Jimmie Rogers picks up the thread.

I was worried about the spot on your Mama's leg. She was worried, too. She was in agony in her bedroom and had a fever. I called Dr. Bruce Bullwinkle. He said to bring her to his office. He wanted to look at it. It was about 4:30 in the afternoon. We went to the back door, and he was waiting for us. He examined the spot and said, "Joan, I am putting you in the hospital." She resisted, said, "I'm going to the party." He said, "No, you're going now to the hospital." I took her to the hospital, then drove to her house and got her gowns and makeup. She never came home again.

Two days later, on August 21st, I visited my mother at the Baptist Memorial Hospital in New Albany. I was saddened by what I saw and heard. The note in my journal said, "She's going down fast, resigned." That night I couldn't sleep. I got up and began writing her obituary and eulogy.

I spent the next morning with Mom, Bill Blizzard, and my brother David. She looked better. The next day, August 24th, I drove over from Tupelo after work. Not a positive scene. She had no color and appeared to be deteriorating. Dr. Jones, her oncologist, had some encouraging words but not many. "You may have her another two weeks." The next day she seemed improved, had her color back, and for the first time I was hopeful she was going to beat this disease. David was, too, and flew back to Iraq. I fed and nursed her and for an-other time in my life with her, experienced that touching *there there*. The next day her improvement continued.

On the August 27th, I thought she was turning the corner. She was angry, combative, and agitated, that centuries-old Ferguson toughness and defiance flaring.

Fergusons and Lamars do not go gently into that good night. They shadow box with death. I think they derive some satisfaction from the combat, eyeballing the reaper and saying, "Not yet. Get the Hell out." Who knows the genetic key, the origin of this defiant syndrome? Mother's oldest brother Guy researched the family tree, traveling even to the Register House in Edinburgh, Scotland, tracing the Fergusons all the way back to the sixth century and Angus McFergus, the first Scottish monarch. Perhaps defiance began with a sheep herder who lay dying, his family called in, only to hear, "Not yet." A couple of days later he was well and back tending his sheep. Or it could have begun in northern France with a Huguenot matriarch or patriarch. Regardless of the lineage, the Ferguson/Lamar family tree was suffused with *"Not yet."*

Josie's mother, Belle Lamar, with each visit of her youngest daughter Martha Glynn from Wichita, Kansas, told everyone that she was dying and would not be alive the next time they came to visit. This ritual was carried out each year the Renickers came and each year, Grandmama Belle would be alive, baking pies, planting jonquils, mending fences. She lived to be 105. I recall her defiance the last year she was alive, waving that cane at anyone who entered her room and telling the funeral director who visited to "Get the hell out." *Not yet*.

Mom's oldest sister, May, was near death several times and each time astonished everyone with remarkable recoveries. In fact, I went to her room at Traceway to say the "last rites." She was moaning and groaning, could not open her eyes, as she lay there in histrionic resignation. That was in early December. On Christmas Eve she attended communion with our family, kneeling and rising unaided from that altar rail at First United Methodist Church in Tupelo. She lived several more years and died at the age of ninety-seven. *Not yet.*

Then there was Josie's brother, Dan.

The joke was told that he died more times than Generalissimo Franco. If you recall from the episodes of the popular show *Laugh In*, it took the Spanish dictator forever to die. In each episode after he died, the actors would say, "And Generalissimo Franco is still dead."

I recall a vacation our family had planned back in the early eighties. Mom called and said, "You can't go now. Your Uncle Dan is dying." We canceled the trip. Uncle Dan didn't die. Two years later, we were scheduled to take a trip to the Smokies. Again, mother called, "Your Uncle Dan is seriously ill. You need to reschedule." We did and Uncle Dan, the quintessential *Not yet*, recovered. The next year, Thanksgiving, 1984, Mom had called and had said Uncle Dan was in critical condition. This time, we were better prepared. We had planned to celebrate Thanksgiving in New Orleans. "We will stop and visit him in Batesville," I told her, "And, if he dies, we'll attend the funeral on the return trip." My *"Not yet!"* uncle did not die. In fact, he lived for another ten years, dying on Sunday March 6, 1994, at the age of 92. I was present in the casket parlor when his son, Danny, the funeral home director, was having difficulty closing his casket and I heard him whisper, "You're stubborn even in death." An appropriate epigram for the Ferguson clan. *Not yet.*

Aunt Ruby, Josie's older sister, suffered multiple illnesses resulting in frequent warnings of imminent death. *Not yet* strung out for several years until her defiant voice was stilled at age 97.

The next sister in line, Blanche, ten years older than my mother, replicated the Not yet mindset! If my Uncle Dan was the king of "Not yet," Aunt Blanche was the queen. At one point, she had congestive heart failure in Gulfport while visiting her daughter Lucy.

While a Peace Corp worker at age 73 (she lied about her age to qualify) in Honduras, she tripped and fell on a sidewalk in Tegucigalpa, busted her patella and had to be medevacked to Penrose Memorial Hospital in Colorado Springs. She survived that injury to return to her home in Michigan City, Mississippi. Soon after she was crawling through tunnels of grass and brush in her pasture, leading a historian and an archeologist to ancient oaks where federal soldiers in Grant's army had carved their names and left messages for sweethearts.

In 2004, the year that my mother died, Aunt Blanche was near death, and the family was called. The note in my journal states, "in serious condition, not expected to live." She died August 25, 2012. She gave the reaper a run for his money. She was 104 years old. If there was any doubt, she was the "Queen of Not yet," January 1st was her birthday. She always approached that date with a sacred sense of conquest … and hopeful continuity.

Then there was Josie.

This story has been passed down for generations. As a young lady, in her early teens, Josie entered a beauty review. The pageant took place in the Cleveland Street Elementary School auditorium. At that time, the stage was slightly elevated, about a foot from the floor. Taking her turn and parading across the stage, Josie fell off the stage and, in her typical indomitable spirit, got back up and continued in the review.

Often, while reflecting upon my mother and her life,

something the French writer Jean Paul Sartre said about William Faulkner comes to mind. He said, "Reading Faulkner was like being a passenger in a moving car, who, instead of looking forward, looks backward at the past hurtling and blurring by, then, with distance, scenery falling lucidly and clearly into place."

I am not a big believer in history. History has no energy. The present is another form of the past, constantly moving, a river into which we step only once. Looking forward is the only viable tense. Yet, only as I look back upon my mother's life blurring by, do I begin to see, with distance and a little detective work, certain episodes and patterns of behavior falling into place.

The year was 1954. I was twelve years old. Letters to my mom and dad from his sisters in Missouri help narrow the time frame. Several focused on the death of my Granddaddy Morris who had died in Trenton, Missouri, in early spring of that year. Dad did not go to the funeral, which I had thought odd, not to go to your own father's funeral. Researching this memoir, I began to recon-struct the pieces of that puzzle. Then I read the following in a letter post-marked May 2:

My dearest Bill,

How is Joan? Surely hope that she is much better and that they have found out what is wrong. Is she still in the hospital …? I do hope that Joan is much improved by this time, Bill. No one can tell us anything about sickness, we have had it now for over a year and a half. I hope the boys are fine. Write to us when you can, we would like to hear how Joan is now. Lots of Love,
    Genevieve

Several months later, Genevieve, my dad's sister, followed up with another note:

Joan,
    Are you still having to wear that awful steel corset for your back? I surely hope you are much better now. No one can tell me anything about how painful a back ailment can be.

Back ailment? Steel corset? Surely more than a back ailment. My mother became deathly ill. She lay on the bed in the middle bedroom for several weeks, moaning and groaning, cold rags on her head. Dr. Bostwick, our family doctor, who lived on the block behind our house, came daily. On one occasion, I recall standing in the hallway overhearing a conversation between my mother and my father. He was sitting on the side of the bed, and I think both had been crying. He had made a comment that he would quit work and come home. "No, Bill. You don't need to do that," she wailed loudly. I heard whispered words "death" and "dying." Hysteria filled the room, spilled over into the house, into my thoughts: *My mother's dying*. I couldn't sleep. I couldn't eat. I refused to go to school. Not because of fear of school, but for fear of what I'd find when I came home—my mother dead. For some reason, in my twelve-year-old mind, teetering between Piaget's concrete and abstract cognitive stages, I reasoned that by staying home, my presence, would stop death. But something else may have stopped death. At that early age, I didn't know what to call it.

Then, as if a holy breeze, a spirit, blew through the house, through the bedroom where she lay, she was up prancing about, headed to the store. In her letter, Genevieve, mentioned back ailment. She might have worn a steel corset, but what I had observed was more than a back problem. I never knew exactly what was wrong with her. The malady or diagnosis was never mentioned. As a psychologist, and again, a psychologist looking through the rear window of that moving car, I see possible hypochondriacal hysteria, conversion disorder or somatoform disorder. Perhaps, some mysterious fever gripped her. I didn't know about menopause at the time, but she was not old enough for that. The greater mystery was not the name of the illness, but the cure, how the disorder went away so quickly. And that was the summer of our epic, three-month trip out west.

Years later, in the mid-nineties, Mother was diagnosed with Coronary Artery Disorder and was told she would have to have open heart surgery. Despite all of our protestations and encouragement and Dr. Max Hutchinson's great track record, she thought then she might die. Then, with Sandi and me holding her hands, Dr. Hutchison said a prayer over her. He was barely through with his prayer and that Ferguson *Not yet* kicked in. "Hell, I'm going to be fine. Y'all get out of here."

I thought of her mother at 105 saying, "Get the hell out." *Not yet*. And my mother was fine, an inspiration to me several years later when I had to undergo the same surgery, same doctor, same hospital.

There was the time, perhaps a year before she died, Mother called me. She said she was very sick and needed to go to the emergency room, in Tupelo, not New Albany. I called a doctor I knew who worked in the ER at North Mississippi Medical Center, and he said he would be prepared to take her in. Jimmie

Rogers drove her, and I went by the next morning. She was concerned she might be dying, but she rallied and was working in her yard two days later.

On August 28, my journal note says, "positive visit with David and Mom ... she's improving. On August 30: "Spent time with Mom, she's still improving, spirits up."

You can understand how I felt history would repeat. The *Not yet*! was coming. It was just around the corner. She was going to fling back those covers, swing those strong legs from that bed and emerge my same Mama Josie saying, *"I'm getting the hell out of here."*

Then the hammer fell. August 31st: "Met with Dr. Jones her oncologist ... bad news ... she may not be around much longer." On September 1, I stayed with her most of the day. I had a book event in Clarksdale the next day. My first published novel, *Land Where My Fathers Died*, was still in demand, and Josie was drawing some pride from its success. On September 3rd, Sandi and I took her some roses. She was able to raise her leg. Anna Katherine, my daughter, was present. We all had a good visit.

In the days that followed, my mom was no better. Sandra Baker Moore arrived from Denver on September 4. On September 6, a nurse from the hospital called. Mom was worse. I cancelled all appointments, rushed to the hospital in New Albany and remained at her side all day and night. Journal notes, "so sad and painful ... we thought we had turned a corner. Granddaughters Meredith and Anna Katherine stayed with me all day. Their husbands, Scott and Joey, in and out."

September 7 was a rough day. I had slept in the room with Mom, but I was up and down all night. The doctors were not encouraging. I began calling family. David was in Iraq and very upset to hear the news. He, too, thought she was turning a corner, that proverbial *Not yet* kicking in again. I guess we all, in those moments, hoped for the *Not yet*. It was painful watching her decline so fast. "I stayed the night again, tired and wiped out ... small miracle: able to get all items from Mom's 3 lockboxes at the bank."

Over the next three days, more family began arriving—David's children, Mom's sister Martha Glynn and her husband Leon, and sister Blanche, Queen of the *Not yet*, hale, and strong at age 96. The last days with Mom were painful, but the nights brought some comfort. I slept in her house, my old home, and reflected on old memories as I worked on her obituary and eulogy.

The last time I saw Mom alive was on September 14. A sheet and blanket were pulled up to her chin. She was heavily sedated, and it seemed she was barely conscious and aware of those around her. I leaned over and said, "I love you, Mom." She responded, her last words to me, "I love you, too, Honey." *There, there*. That evening, I sat on her front porch sharing stories with Bill Blizzard, both of us aware she might not make it through the night.

At 8:10 a.m., David called from the hospital. Mom was much worse, and he was, "afraid she's near the end." I jumped up, dressed hurriedly, and raced to the hospital. As I entered the room, Mom had just flat-lined. The time was 8:20. All of us in the room—Blanche, Martha Glynn, Leon, and David wept and hugged. I asked everyone to gather around the bed and hold hands for a prayer.

Shortly after, Anna Katherine came and walked with me as I accompanied Mom's body to the hearse, my hand constantly on her still warm body. Standing there behind the hearse, watching her body disappear behind its dark doors, my vision swept the area behind the hospital and the ironies began falling into place: The vacant lot where my mother's childhood home had stood. The hickory tree in the front yard, the thick grape vines looping from it where she had swung. The pecan grove in the side yard. The peach, apple, and pear trees in the back. The realization hit me. My mother died in a hospital that stood on the playground of her youth.

Walking back into the hospital, a black lady passed Anna Katherine and me in the hall and said, "The hat lady has died." The woman did not know me, but she certainly knew Josie. She knew the Hat Lady.

As the minister in the family, the mantel fell upon me to assist in conducting her funeral and giving her eulogy.

The funeral was set for the following Saturday 11:00 a.m. at First United Methodist Church. Her casket rested at the chancel, where my father's had rested, the same spot where she had joined the church and received her first Bible, where she and my father had exchanged vows, where my brother and I had been baptized, where I had knelt and made my decision to enter the ministry, beneath the choir loft where she had sung.

The funeral was a celebration. Hats ruled the day. All of the female family members, nieces, and daughters-in-law, raided Mom's hat closet, and each wore one of her stylish, wide-brimmed hats. A flaming red hat sat atop the casket.

Along with her pastors, Rev. Giles Lindsey and Rev. Leslie Nabors, I officiated. I sat by her casket from 10:00 to 11:00 as she lay in state in the sanctuary of her church, First United Methodist Church, until the service began. The eulogy was a "Hat's Off" tribute to a classy woman of style and dash and daring. I thought it appropriate to incorporate it into these final pages of her memoir.

Figure 30. All the "girls" wearing Mom's hats

Figure 31. David and I, holding the red hat that was placed atop her casket

Chapter 19: Eulogy
Joan Ferguson Morris
1918-2004

Where does one begin to describe or define Joan Ferguson Morris? I was struggling with the question when I recalled what the lady had said when we were leaving the hospital: "The hat lady is dead."

Joan Ferguson Morris was a woman who wore hats.

She was a woman who wore many different hats.

She wore hats that had a flair about them.

She wore hats that had color.

She wore hats that were vibrant.

She wore hats that brought a touch of drama to a room, to a gathering.

She wore hats that were attractive, caught your eye.

She wore hats that had style, class … elegance.

She wore hats with character.

She wore hats with personality.

She wore hats that defined who she was.

And today our hats are off to you, Mom.

Our hats are off to you for the tender care and devotion rendered unto your own mother in her final years and days, providing us that memorable role model.

Hats off to you for laying a spiritual foundation from which we could draw for years to come, for daily morning devotionals and blessings at mealtimes, for these rituals that keep us on track.

Hats off, too, for the values you instilled, for remarking once to a lady when she said that integration was destroying our southern way of life, you said, "But in heaven there is no southern way of life." I recall something David shared with me that LC, the young black man Mom shepherded along the way, had said: "White or black, makes no difference, Miss Joan will take you down."

Hats off to you, too, for being such a remarkable model of success and drive and achievement and entrepreneurship, for challenging us to become better than we are, to become more than the sum of our parts.

Hats off to you for dragging us kicking and screaming into the world of music and piano lessons, for pushing us in scouting and wearing proudly on a bracelet you designed, the eagle pins for mothers.

Hats off to you for instilling us with a sense of adventure, an openness and a zest for life, a love for travel, for steering us into worlds beyond our own. If there is one scripture that encapsulates Joan Ferguson Morris, it is this one from the Gospel of John: "I came that you should have life and have it more abundantly."

Hats off to you for your thirst of knowledge, for having an interest in everything under the sun, for being, in every sense of the word, a true Renaissance woman, a woman for all seasons. For who else has, at one time or another, besides selling jewelry and watches and china, also had a hat shop, a dress shop, a flower shop, sold pianos and furniture and antiques and the list goes on. Who else did all that and took a correspondence course and became a self-taught interior decorator? Hats off to you for the versatility, for the many hats you wore in our lives, in our community. Hats off to the memory of all those many hats.

Hats off for the jokes and stories you told that brought laughter to a room, and for that added dimension, standing and prancing around, acting them out.

Hats off to the flowers you grew, especially the perennials. They, in particular, will remind us most of you.

Hats off to the legacy of friendship you leave, the importance of friends and loyalty and not to grow old without them.

Hats off for the wisdom to know, and to choose, two good Bills and give each the best years of their lives.

And finally, hats off for the dignity you brought to death. You endured with grace under pressure.

I could go on and on, but we'd be here till the cows come home. That's the best we can do for now. But I will write about you someday, Mother, in a big way. About a classy lady. A class act ... in a class all her own.

And she's causing a hubbub in heaven right now. Can't you just see her, sashaying through those pearly gates, and every angel and archangel, male or female, stumbling over each other's feet to exchange halos for a hat.

As bankrupt as our vocabularies are in this moment, there is one phrase, one word, that says it all. Steel magnolia doesn't come close. Nor does Iron Lady. Unsinkable maybe approximates. But the one word that comes to mind, that evokes the best of the best of all of the above? The indomitable, enduring, classy "Hat Lady."

Following the committal, everyone returned to the church for a parade of hats and a celebratory meal.

Figure 32. Late 90's photo of Mom with Olivia, David, Jonathan, and Daniel standing

Chapter 20: Epilogue

As I write her memoir on the anniversary of her death, September 15, 2018, had she lived, had leukemia microbes not invaded her body, she would have been one hundred years old, or young. Reflecting on her life, I think often of a musical I was in when a senior at Millsaps College: The *Unsinkable Molly Brown*. When it came to tough times and situations, she stood her ground. There was something almost British about her, the stiff upper lip, the over-articulated voice, the drilling stare. Like her father and mother and *all* of her siblings, and I mean all of them, she was tough with class, even when she was wrong. Except for the leukemia microbe that invaded her strong body, she was indestructible. She was *Sarge*.

Joan "Josie" Ferguson Morris left a deep footprint of pioneer spirit, hard work, perseverance, persistence, and endurance. "Steel magnolia"? I don't think so. Too trite and overused. Gold or silver or platinum magnolia? Too simple. She had multiple personas, many personalities, manifold talents. She was eclectic, diversified and myriad. The analogy of a kaleidoscope comes to mind. When you peer through its tiny hole, you see a world of multiple-colored fragments, some large and some small. As you turn the tube, everything shifts, and you try to keep your eye on the big pieces. But there were other, smaller but distinct pieces, clustered around the larger ones.

Josie was as multi-faceted, as hard, and as flashy as the precious gem she sold, wore, and loved. My Mama Josie was all diamond.

Today the land I remember on Marshall Hill and the old

home place is occupied by Baptist Memorial Hospital, several fast-food restaurants, Walgreen's, a gardening nursery, and a Huddle House. A few of the peach, apple, pear, and pecan trees can be seen, but most of my grandfather's prize orchard has been taken over by concrete and glass. Also, still visible in season are the jonquils my grandmother planted along with clusters of irises, canna, multi-colored day lilies and ferns. Some I dug up years ago and transplanted in my mother's yard in New Albany and mine in Tupelo where they still bloom each spring. The blackberry and dewberry vines that had extended north toward Highway 30 are gone. Due west of where the house had been, where my grandfather had his cane syrup mill amid a field of cotton, A four-lane highway cuts a wide swath and west of it are strip malls and a Lowes, a Walmart, and Mexican and fast-food restaurants.

All of that land had been mine and my mother's playground for the time she lived there and the years members of the family lived in the house. Following my grandparents' deaths, my Aunt May retired from teaching and lived in the house. It stayed in the family and at one point was moved by my brother to a nearby location where it still stands. The land was eventually, through a long drawn out and contentious process, sold to the government for the Highway 78 four-lane bypass that would become Interstate 22.

Each time I drive through New Albany on Interstate 22, I pass by the old home place. I see the two hickory trees, the vine still hanging from one, and the pecan trees, and I think of another era. Of playing ball in a large yard now overgrown. Of a barn and smokehouse, a chicken coop and hog pen, all long gone. Images come to mind of my grandmother rhythmically churning butter and mixing lard and pig fat with lye in a huge black cauldron to make soap. Traveling in the west lane on Interstate 22, I drive directly over the spot once occupied by my grandfather's sorghum molasses operation, over the exact location of a copse of woods where my mother and her sisters played, where she hid the night she told everyone she had poured milk into the well.

I think of those times of hardship, of crop failures and the Great Depression, of an almost unimaginable primitive existence and a pioneer spirit pervading it. I think of an unsophisticated simple time and the lives that emerged from it, were nurtured by it. I think of my Grandmama Lamar and my Granddaddy Ferguson, of their austere and humble beginnings. I think of my uncles and aunts.

I think of a diamond who emerged from that small red-clay dirt farm.

I think of my mother.

I think of Josie.

Appendix A: Ferguson Siblings Bios

Guy Montgomery, the first and eldest son of Jake and Susie Belle Ferguson, was born June 6, 1895. He grew up in the log cabin in Etta. When he was old enough, he took over some of the chores delegated by his father. He attended the nearby school of Mt. Erin to the 8th grade, as far as he could go there, then transferred to New Albany where he attended school in the winter months and obtained his diploma. He excelled in track and at Field Day, his senior year, he won awards in pole vaulting and broad jump. Following his graduation from high school that spring, Guy went to work at a brick kiln southeast of New Albany.

While at home that summer, Guy demonstrated his genius at carpentry. Blanche describes the playground equipment he made for the children in the Marshall Hill neighborhood:

> He made a swing under one of the big oak trees down near the well. He took a sapling with a diameter of three or four inches, split it about 8 feet up, put a board for the seat at the split end of the sapling, forcing it between the split ends and fastening it with nails driven in. A chain was run through the top and fastened to the big limb above. This was the greatest swing of all times—and so ingenious of Brother Guy to make such.

Blanche goes on to describe his other playground equipment constructions: "He made us playground equipment that has not been heard or seen before or after. We were the only people outside of the city park that had a giant slide, a flying jenny, a swing, and a seesaw. (See Appendix H)

According to Blanche's journal notes, Guy left home when she was in 2nd grade to work for Roger Wilson, An Englishman who was a cotton buyer in Memphis. "This was the year 1916. On April 7, 1917, President Wilson declared war on the Axis. Guy was gone before June. He had volunteered. He came home from Ft. Oglethorpe in September and by October was in Europe."

Upon his return home from WWI, on September 21, 1919, Guy married Emma Lorena McCurry. He had heard of a job in south Mississippi with a lumber industry, Gilchrist Timber. Jones County, Mississippi had a history of its own, certainly one that would appeal to a young adventurer seeking his own life. Jones County had the distinction of seceding from the Confederacy and fighting its own war against both sides in the Civil War. Jones County was noted for its timber, not its cotton, and had no interest in joining Confederate forces. A man there named Gilchrist had built a timber industry, liked young Ferguson's grit, and welcomed him aboard.

Figure 33. Guy and Lorena in Oregon

At some point, Guy left Gilchrist and went to work as an auditor for the government and moved all over the south before heading west. His grandson and namesake, Guy, provided the following information: 1933—Norfolk, Virginia; 1934—Nashville, Tennessee, Washington, D. C., and Skyline Drive, Virginia;1938—New Albany, Mississippi; 1940—Austin and San Antonio, Texas. About this time, Mr. Gilchrist decided to move his sprawling timber operation from Jones County to Oregon and prevailed upon Guy to return to work for him. Guy played a major role in the transition and became general manager for the Gilchrist-Timber Railroad. My family and I visited him there in 1954 on our legendary trip out West. I was astonished at his leadership and courage. In that winter climate, amid heavy snowfall, he would ride the timber trains up front, eyeful for fallen trees across the tracks. Aunt Emma said, "I can't sleep at night when he goes out on those trains. He's been thrown twice."

Figure 34 Photo of Guy

Emma died September 20, 1965, and Guy married her sister, Maude Barkley April 17, 1966. Before his death in 1976, Guy lived down the street from our house and I would stop and visit frequently and listen to his stories. On Christmas Day, 1976, Guy had a heart attack. The attack was not fatal, not at that time. My mother and my brother, David, and I stopped by the next morning on our way out of town to check on him. Mother wanted to cash in on sales at Goldsmith's. When we entered his room, Guy was sitting up, alert and joking. He said

Figure 35 Guy with Gilchrist Lumber in Oregon, circa. 1950

the doctor had said he'd had a light heart attack and needed to stay in the hospital a few days for observation. We left, drove to Memphis, shopped and on return stopped by the Union County Hospital, which sat on the same grounds where he had made the playground equipment, the same where Mom had played. I went up the elevator ahead of Mom and David. No one was in the room. The bed was empty. I got on the elevator to return to the ground floor where David met me. "He died," David said.

Anna May Ferguson was born May 23, 1897. She attended school at Mt. Erin, near the Ferguson Galway home, to the 8th grade and transferred behind Guy, who was two years ahead of her, to New Albany. Upon graduation from New Albany High School, she attended Blue Mountain College and obtained her teaching degree. She returned to New Albany, where she could live at home, and taught in the high

Figure 36. May Ferguson

school where she had graduated. At some point, during the Great Depression, May was teaching in Cartersville, Georgia. These were tough times and she agreed to pay Blanche's room and board which was $18 per month. Blanche writes, "I really didn't want her to do that, so I borrowed $100 from Will McGill, the owner of the Coca Cola Bottling works. Then I tutored a fifth-grade child every afternoon an hour five days a week and got $500 a week for that. May came up anyway with board money many of the months and sent me one beautiful navy-blue georgette dress, longer than the very short ones before the Depression hit."

How long May taught at New Albany High School is unknown but at some point, she left home and moved to Hickory Flat. She taught there and at Potts Camp. She never learned to drive. I recall the long drives my mother made, picking her up and bringing her home on weekends. When I obtained my driver's license, that became my weekend chore, driving Aunt May. I'd pick her up at my Grandmamas, take her to buy her groceries and shop and take her back. Often, I'd ride with my mother to pick her up in Potts Camp or Hickory Flat and take her home. My mother never complained. Eventually, Aunt May moved to Forrest City, Arkansas, and taught school there for a long time. Sometime around 1957, she retired and moved back home to care for my grandmother who, at that time, was in Graceland Nursing Home, about a mile from her home.

As though she was on a mission, May visited my grandmother daily, often walking the distance there and back. She never married, had no children, and it seemed that taking care of her mother was not only what was expected of her, but her duty. Her dedication was unparalleled and inspiring. When asked by Blanche why she never married, May said, "I was really crazy about the men in the area, but I didn't marry any of them because they never asked." When her friend Swift Rogers posed the same question, May gave this classic response: "My father told me never to settle for common stock, only blue chip—but blue chip never came along."

Occasionally, I would spend the night in the old home with her, to provide some company for her. I felt she must be lonely. And, if truth be told, I needed a break from my mother who was in her control mode. Then I had an epiphany: *There's just as many weeds over there as there is over here.* Control ran in the family, I decided. Aunt May hovered over me like a mother hen.

But during those times, and the times I chauffeured her around, Aunt May and I learned some things about each other. She appeared to notice, or accept, that I was growing up with interests similar to hers. I witnessed her tireless and dedicated care of my grandmother, her toleration of aloneness … and her intelligence. The books in her library were impressive: Balzac, Chaucer, Proust, Montaigne—foreign names I had never heard. Where did this desire to read them originate, from what corner of her early log cabin world? From what tidbit she might have picked up in a very rural beginning? What teacher? What person? What gene? There were also works by Faulkner, F. Scott Fitzgerald, Hemingway. In those days of youth, I recognized only the name Faulkner, mainly because my mother's best friend, Kate Baker, lived in Oxford next door to Rowan Oak and we would visit frequently, driving over the then graveled Highway 30. I began to pull these books from their shelves and read. It was my first acquaintance with great literature. Later, before she died, she gave the books to me.

They now grace the shelves of my library and will be passed along to my children and theirs. Those books would pull me back to that house to spend afternoons on the porch glider reading, absorbing … learning.

One other thing I learned about my Aunt May that shocked me. She always wore her hair pulled up in a coiled bun. I thought it was because she was supposed to look like a teacher, and it went with the job. That may have been the case. But there was another reason. When I stayed with her, I slept in the front bedroom where her dressing table was located. One night I had climbed into bed early to read and observed her taking down her hair. It went down, and down, and down … all the way to the floor. I was awestruck. I asked her why she let it grow so long.

"I just don't cut my hair," she responded.

"Why?" I pressed.

"Not sure, Edd. I guess I'm just attached to it."

The next morning, she left before I awoke, walked the mile, or so trek to Graceland and to her mother.

After my Grandmama's death in 1978, May moved into town, into a duplex apartment on Cleveland Street a block down from our house. I had earned my doctorate in psychology from Ole Miss and was working with a mental health center in Corinth and I received a call one evening from my mother: "Edd, we had to put your Aunt May in the hospital."

"What's wrong?"

She described a series of incidents involving bizarre behavior, throwing bricks through windows, chasing children. In short, my mother was calling me for help. Baptist Memorial Hospital in New Albany had transferred her to a hospital in Memphis, a place called Lakeside. I was new to my profession and had never heard of it.

"But that's not the first mental hospital she's been in," my mother continued. "She's been in St. Francis. No one has been able to help her."

She asked if I would call Lakeside, which I did, and spoke to a psychiatrist who would become a best friend of our family's and a great help for my future clients. His name is Radwan Haykal. He is a Muslim and one of the most caring, healing people I have ever known. He is also a magician with medication. Within two days he had my Aunt May stabilized. Within a week, she was back in her apartment on Cleveland Street as though nothing had happened.

"Depakote," Dr. Haykal said. "It works beautifully with agitation in geriatric populations."

May remained in New Albany for a few more years then we moved her to Traceway United Methodist Retirement Center in Tupelo where I could keep a closer eye on her. One of the last things I did for her was take her to the Christmas Eve Communion Service at First United Methodist Church in Tupelo. I thought she would enjoy the music and the service. But she was restless and ready to leave. She wanted to, "go back to my room." Reflecting on that near catastrophic evening, I see more clearly now. She wanted to return to her aloneness, to her solitary life.

Ultimately, she died on August 24, 1989. Through the United Methodist Scholarship Fund, I established honoring her, The Anna May Ferguson Scholarship Fund to this day is still growing and used by deserving students seeking an education. I get a monthly report and fondly think of my Aunt May, her dedication to learning, her dedication to her mother … and to her hair.

Ruby Sue was born October 9, 1899. She spent her early years growing up in the log cabin at Rocky Ford with Guy and May and attended the Mt. Erin school until the family moved to New Albany. She was, arguably, the most gifted of the Ferguson brood. Living in the log cabin, she played the organ, wrote poetry, and developed into a culinary specialist. A cousin, Tommy Lamar, wrote his Ole Miss masters English thesis on her poetry. She graduated from New Albany High School and obtained her college degree from Blue Mountain College with a major in English.

Blanch remembers:
I was my sister Ruby's charge and I called her "B." She seemed to do more for me than anyone else, showed more affection and petted me. I can't recall Mama paying much attention or doing much more than cooking and sewing. May was there but nothing in my first four years do I remember, nor do I remember my brother Guy. First grade passed by without anything very memorable happening. I peed in my pants one day but got over that without any trouble. I think Ruby was sent for and I was allowed to stand over the register until I got dry.

On December 28, 1920, Ruby made one of the smartest decisions of her life and married John Nesbit Grace. The location of their first home in New Albany is unknown. Their second home, the one I remember, was a nice brick house on North Street between Cleveland Street Elementary School and Highland Street. Their three children, John, Jean, and Betty grew up in that home.

My Mama Josie, Martha Glynn and Blanche would spend the night with Ruby and Nesbit and attend the Ritz Theater where Blanche worked in the ticket office. Nesbit liked the movies, and he would walk them to and from "the picture show." Jean and Betty were campus beauties at Mississippi State College for Women and attracted standout football players from Mississippi State. John Grace had something to do with that. I recall playing with Jess Hughes (who married Jean) and Bob Jefferies (who married Betty) and Billy "Spook" Murphy who was a friend of both Jess and John.

My Aunt Ruby motivated in strange and intriguing ways. I was in her home one day. I remember it was late spring. I had almost flunked out of Ole Miss and she was on my case. "You're behind your class," she said standing in the kitchen slapping a long spatula in the palm of her hand. "You're retarded." That was a painful moment in my life. In a fit of anger, I stomped through her house, Nesbit calling me to come back. But it was a good anger burn. From that point forward in my education, I achieved honor rolls. I was determined to prove to Aunt Ruby that I was not retarded.

When she died January 14, 1991, I felt honored to be asked to conduct her funeral.

Dan Lamar was born December 6, 1901, in Galway. He attended school at Mt. Erin until the eighth grade and graduated from New Albany High School. When old enough, Dan helped Guy with the farm chores and spent some of his time creating mischief and anxieties for his sisters. Blanche notes that he would tell her about "Raw and Bloody Bones" that were in the barn, and she stayed away.

Early on, Dan was a deal maker. Blanche tells this story:

Every chance I had I took a ride on our mule George, every day after school or in the summer. There was one hitch—the jersey bull was in the same pasture with George. Every time I set foot in that pasture that bull with head down started pawing and inching toward me. Dan caught him once or twice for me, but decided it was taking some of his milking time, so we made a deal. If I would learn to milk two cows every night, he would catch George for me every afternoon. I hopped at this. It didn't take me but a few minutes to catch on to that rhythm of milking. Thus, a bargain was made. So, every afternoon I would saddle George and start out.

On November 16, 1930, Dan married Irene Elizabeth Dickens, perhaps one of the smartest decisions of his life. How and where Dan met Irene Dickens is not known, but apparently it happened in Batesville. By marriage, Dan inherited Dickens Funeral Home and successfully ran it along with a plantation and cattle ranch over the Batesville bridge in the Mississippi Delta. I recall that Irene's reclusive mother, Mrs. Dickins, lived on the second floor of the home which probably belonged to her as did the funeral home.

Whether it was a "presence of mind" thing or true love, or both, Jake, and Susie Belle's fourth child and second son married into money and became a good custodian of the windfall. He also became an astute and adroit politician. Seven years after his marriage, he was elected mayor of Batesville, a position he held from 1937 until 1951 when he filled the unexpired term of Senator John Kyle serving as State Senator from the 33rd District, until 1953. He returned as mayor in

1953 and served until 1973 for a total of 35 years in that elected position.

Figure 37 Dan and Irene

During his term as mayor of Batesville, the first paved streets were constructed. Dan was instrumental in establishing the Tallahatchie Valley Electric Power Association as Batesville became the site of the TVA headquarters and later became the first municipality in the state served by a private utility to receive a certificate of convenience and necessity to construct an electric distribution system. Also, during his tenure as mayor, Batesville received its first certificate of need from the State A & I Board to permit the building of an industry for the city resulting in the Batesville Company. He also worked for the reactivation and relocation of the Northwest Mississippi Livestock Association barn and show in Batesville. He was instrumental in locating the Highway District Office in Batesville. Overall improvements were made in the city's infrastructure including a new library and fire department.

During his tenure, Batesville was the first city on the Tennessee Gas Transmission line to receive permission to construct a city owned gas system.

Dan Ferguson was president of the Executive Committee of the Mississippi Municipal Association in 1970-71 and for 20 years was a voting delegate to the National League of Cities. He was an active member of First United Methodist Church (where I preached once with him sitting on the front row).

He was a doting son and came to New Albany often to see his mother. He would come to my parent's jewelry store. His chauffeur would always park in front of the store and Dan would emerge from the Cadillac, always dressed in a vested suit with diamond stick pin and carrying, not using, a gold-handled walking cane, all of this somewhat flamboyancy topped with a wide-brimmed white planter's hat. He would take up court at the rear of the store in a cane back chair, sitting erect, hands folded over the top of the cane and tell stories to the onlookers who had seen the Cadillac and gathered around expecting another round from the consummate raconteur. He spoke in a high-pitched whiny quavering voice, like my grandfather's. And he could tell some of the funniest and most unbelievable stories.

There was one that circulated through the family. My mother said I should write about it, but I could never get enough information. It occurred during the depression. My Uncle Dan was driving from New Albany to Batesville, through Oxford, on Highway 30. He came across a wrecked car but no one in it. He searched the area and found a man under some bushes clutching a money bag. Dan knew the man who worked at the then Bank of Commerce in New Albany. He was taking a bag of money to a bank in Oxford and his car skidded off the road. It had been raining slightly. The man feared leaving the scene of an accident, so he gave the bag of money to Dan to deliver to the Oxford bank. I never heard the end of the story. My uncle, being a man of integrity, probably delivered the money. But my mother always said, each time the story was told that, "there's more to that tale."

One story can be confirmed. I do not know, and do not recall the details. There was a big political Democratic event that took place in Batesville. Many state dignitaries were present, including Governor J. P. Coleman. My Aunt Irene was too embarrassed to even acknowledge that the event occurred. Apparently, Dan and the governor got into a shouting match about something, and Dan invited Governor Coleman to leave the balcony where they were standing and fight it out in the yard below. Governor Coleman refused. Nothing further was said of the matter.

A final comment on my Uncle Dan. On one occasion, several of us—my grandmother, a few cousins, my mother—were sitting around my grandmother's dining room table. Uncle Dan commenced telling tales. He was mid-tale and stopped. He had seen me taking notes and said, in that high whiney voice, "I'm not telling anymore stories, I'm gonna to write my own damn book." And he told no more. I should have been more discreet. He never wrote the book.

Robbie Pearl was born on October 10, 1903. Once old enough, she fell into the line of routines. According to Blanche, Robbie's chores were to sterilize the discs from the separator, fill lamps with oil and keep lamp chimneys polished.

She was also the wit and court jester of the crowd and didn't miss an opportunity to wise-crack. An example: When younger, a friend of the family's, Louis Kelly, was fat and slow on his feet and no one wanted him on their team. He and Robbie were the same age. Once, when they were teammates, he missed a play and Robbie shouted, "Louis Kelly, you're not worth a fart!" She was ordered to leave the yard.

Robbie graduated from New Albany High School. On a business scholarship, she attended Bowling Green University. On February 7. 1930, she married James Forrest Short, a Memphis businessman who owned several businesses including a grocery store, two restaurants and a janitorial service. Robbie worked at Sears in Memphis for several years and quit when she became pregnant.

Willie Blanche, the sixth Ferguson child and my mother's older sister was born January 1, 1908. She spent her early years in the log house at Etta before moving to Marshall Hill. Around 1927, she graduated from New Albany High School where she recalled, "walking a mile and a half to and from school, weather permitting and when the weather was bad Papa took the surrey." She attended Mississippi State College for Women (MSCW) where her major was Political Science. When the depression hit her junior year, she got a teaching job. She had no teaching credentials and had to take a teaching exam. She passed and got a job teaching near her first home in Etta at the Pinedale Community teaching seventh and eighth grade English. After six months, the school board met with all of the teachers to tell them the money had played out. The students needed two more months. The community rallied around the teachers, boarded, and fed them.

Blanche saved enough money that year to go to summer school in Memphis and take education courses to avoid having to take the teaching exam again. During those two months, she dated Bill Stepp who played baseball for the New York Giants and was a student from Memphis State Teachers College. She learned to play the cello so she could get into MSTC and at one point played with the University Symphony Orchestra.

Figure 38 Photo of Blanche

Blanche taught at Center School, in the eastern part of the county five miles from New Albany, where her main delight was, "Walking through the woods four miles to Wallerville every day for our mail and our buying a bar of candy and having a nice visit with the postmistress." At Center School she taught biology, "without any kind of lab," she wrote in her memoirs. In 1934, Blanche obtained her degree from MSCW, and studied at the American College of Physical Education in Chicago.

At some point in the late 1930's, after relationships with a number of prominent men, she met and married Marvin Treadwell Aldrich. The marriage was short lived because he died December 15, 1945. She outlived him by 67 years and never remarried. He was a cattleman and rancher from Michigan City, Mississippi, where she settled in for the remainder of her life until she died in 2012.

During the remaining 67 years of her life, Blanche was the principal of the Oxford Elementary School in Oxford, Mississippi, (where she ran CBS news reporter Dan Rather from the grounds during the Meredith upheaval in 1962). She taught and served as principal with the U. S. Armed Forces schools in Bamburg, Germany and Madrid, Spain, traveled the world over using freighters as her main conveyance (which was inexpensive and always an adventure). Blanche lied about her age and joined the Peace Corps with a brief stint in Honduras (until she broke her patella) eventually returning to her home in Michigan City. She remodeled the small clapboard schoolhouse where she had taught, named it Twin Oaks for the two large oak trees bracketing the entrance (one called George, the other Martha) and began a long tradition of celebrating Flag Day on June 14 with pomp and ceremony. People traveled long distances to attend, and participate, in the event. At age ninety, she had her driver's license renewed, allowing her to continue cruising Mississippi and Tennessee roads in her yellow Volkswagen and wearing her safari hat and yellow scarf.

She died August 25, 2012. She was 104 years old, one year shy of her mother's legacy. I had the honor of delivering her eulogy.

Figure 39. Blanche Mounting a Horse

Martha Glynn, the ninth and youngest of the siblings, was born February 27, 1920, in New Albany, Mississippi. She graduated from New Albany High School in 1938 and attended business school in Austin Texas for two years. On October 7, 1942, at Randolph Field, Texas, she married Leon J. Renicker. While Leon served in the Army overseas, she moved back to New Albany. Their first son, Leon J. Renicker, Jr, was born January 6, 1944, in New Albany. After Leon's military service, the couple moved to Wichita, Kansas where Leon worked as a typesetter for McCormick Printing Company.

While living in Wichita, Martha Glynn worked for a doctor's group and retired from the City of Wichita/Sedgwick County Health Department in 1980. She and Leon resided in Wichita until 1985 when Leon retired, and they moved to Colorado Springs. Martha and Leon had two more children—John Lamar born July 27, 1946, and Julie Glynn born January 30, 1948.

Figure 40. Siblings May, Robbie, Blanche, Joan, Martha Glynn

Martha enjoyed gardening and was the consummate affirmer to her nephews and nieces. Following a lengthy off and on battle with cancer, Martha Glynn Ferguson Renicker was taken by the disease that also claimed the life of her sister Joan and died March 23, 2006. She was 86 years old, the same age as Josie when she died. Appendix B

Figure 41. Early family reunion on the old place in New Albany

Figure 42 Last Full Reunion, Sardis Lake, Before 2004

Appendix B: Growing Up on Marshall Hill
By Blanche Aldrich

Before our little group on the Hill got into the terrible teens, we were very busy without main activities when we were not in school.

When we were in school, we never saw each other, and if we did, we treated each other as strangers. Generations apart. We had our classmates.

Home base was different. Usually, we would go for horseback rides. None of us had bicycles. The girls had just about put paper dolls away. Jumping off the barn had given way to other deals. We did find fun in hide and seek and had our own counting games for the one who was "it."

To find the initial "it", was the chant of "eenie meenie, mighty mo, catch a rabbit by its toe. It if hollers," etc. I am "it" in this first play. The one who comes out on "it" counts and seeks first.

His chant: Last night, night before twenty-four robbers at my door. I got up, let one in. Hit in the head with a rolling pin. A bushel of corn, a bushel of rye. All ain't hid, holler "I." A bushel of wheat, a basket of clover. All ain't hid can't hide over. Here I would come with both eyes open.

Home base was where he was chanting, when "it" started out to hunt. Those that could came running home. The one he found first became "it" and the game goes on.

Red Rover was another. Whoever on the side who dared to come over when the chant from the opposite side sounded out "Red Rover, Red Rover, let one of theirs come over."

The challenger came charging over full force to break the chain, holding hands in a clutching manner, tried to break through. This game could be very dangerous, and parents would not let us play it. "Run water, run take two steps. Stop, water, stop, take two steps." This meant as "it" nears you, you can take two steps to avoid "it." The one caught becomes "it."

Living statures: It takes one by the right hand and with a gentle swing, turns the player around. The player leaves his hands in the position as it is released and the body the same. After all, had participated, "it" decides on the best stature, a new "it" continues.

For quiet games, we found a concrete walk and played jacks, sometimes marbles. Stealing sticks could involve all ages. Equal number of players on each side of an imaginary line. Equal distance from center line on each side a pile of ten sticks were placed in the center, four guards stood online, the others in the background. The players tried to break through and pick up sticks in opponent's pile. If they get caught and stay in prison at the stick pile until someone pulls him out. The team emptied the opponents' stick pile.

Later, more organized games came along. Baseball or softball with a homemade ball. When the Ed McAllisters' Uncle Dee came to visit them, he started football for us. Miss Ora, his sister, chided him about having the young ladies take part. Then we found other things.

Every early summer, we got ready to go on our overnight trek to Tallahatchie River. We had our own style of packs, utensils for cooking for Ruth, who was the youngest. We had these all tied in her knap sack that contained her pillow. The blanket contained all. The rest of us had cards and other games and the foods for our midnight meal and breakfast. The sandwiches and apples were for the midnight meal.

Getting there was the most difficult of all. Roy, Daniel, and Fred told us they knew a short cut. So, we fell for that. They took us through a deep marsh with deep tall vegetation that we should not have gone through. Our feet sank so deep in the mud that we could not get them out only by taking our feet and manipulating by pulling the shoe out. We managed to hold each on to each other to get free.

Finally, the bank was reached and preparation for the long night had started. We fussed about such a hard trip it was getting through that marsh and among the tall bushes. Those sat back and had a big laugh. It was not a short cut but was the most fun for them they had ever had.

We sat and ate sandwiches and our food that we had in a bag of ice. Then, to our surprise, they had brought a pack of cigarettes, which we all lit up and smoked, feeling very wicked. Jokes, stories, and big lies were told, making them up as they went along. Our old quilts were spread finally and most of us slept by bits, and we rolled up in quilts or blankets.

Morning came early and fires were made. Bacon and scrambled eggs have never tasted so good. Our trip home was easier for the back packs were lighter. We found the shorter and easier path home. We girls got together and declared we would fill the boys' sandwiches with pepper the next year.

We gradually grew up a bit the next year. I had come after my freshman year at MSCW in Columbus, Mississippi. Daniel and Louise had graduated from New Albany High School. Julia, Roy, and Fred were trailing. Virginia was to graduate next, and Ruth was in the eighth grade.

That summer, Daniel had driver's license and we had an easier time. I don't think we ever had as much fun. Our interest were very very different and we later went our separate ways.

Appendix C: Depression Days 1929-1932

I was a Junior at the Mississippi State College for Women when the news of the Big Depression had hit us.

My father was a small farm owner. He had two families on the place who were renting some of the cotton land. Cotton prices had climbed to $.88 per pound. Papa wanted to wait until it reached $1.00 per pound. At settling up time with the tenants, he tried to get them to wait too, but they wanted to sell right then so Papa bought their cotton at $.88 per pound. All the cotton raised on the farm, fifty bales, were Papa's lot. BANG! Everyone was hit hard. His bales were in storage for ten years, then sold for ten cents per pound was about the cost of storage.

Heads got together; my school days looked as if they would be over at the end of the first semester. May, my oldest sister, was teaching in Cartersville, Georgia. She agreed to pay my board which was $18 per month. I really didn't want her to do that, so I borrowed $100.00 from Will Magill, the owner of Coca Cola Bottling Works. Then I tutored a fifth-grade child every afternoon an hour five days a week and got $5.00 a week for that. May came up anyway with board money many of the months and sent me one beautiful navy-blue georgette dress, longer than the very short ones before the Depression hit.

Which reminds me that dresses had gotten very short, above the knee, in fact. We had a song there at school that we sang:

> *Eve was immodest 'til she ate that apple*
> *That old apple was to blame, for the moment that she ate it*
> *She became humiliated, so she hit behind the apple tree*

'Til darkness came
If that one apple made the first girl modest
It will do that as well as then
For if the mothers let their daughters wear their dresses any shorter
We're going to pass those apples around again.

That school year over, I knew full well I would have to look for a teaching job. Along in summer, my father scouted around and found me one sixteen miles from New Albany where we lived on the outskirts.

The school was Pinedale Community in Etta, Mississippi. There were two churches in that area, the Baptist church at Bethel and the Methodist at Salem. Pinedale was about halfway between.

My major in college was Political Science and I had aimed at Geneva or at The Hague. My sister was there that summer and gave me good suggestions and ideas. Since I didn't have any credential for teaching. I had to take a teacher's exam. It was crucial but I made it.

Papa found a place for me to board where I paid $15.00 a month rooming with two other teachers. One was an experienced teacher. She had first, second and third grades downstairs at school. The other, Effie, nearer my age who was my bed fellow taught fourth, fifth, and sixth grades. She was downstairs. I taught seventh and eighth grade English. There was no twelfth grade.

A whole page should be written about the building. It was a frame building, a big boy, with four rooms on the first floor with a wide hall between two rooms on each side, then the arrangement on the second. The principal was Mr. Tutor whose first name has faded away. We didn't every use it. He taught Math to the seventh, eighth, ninth, tenth and eleventh grades, then history also. No, I had History, English, Geography for the seventh and eighth grades. There was a thirty-minute recess with no bell. He got out and hollered "Books, books," to corral the student body in. I loathed that so I got a tin bucket and a stick and beat on it. The building had been there many years, but it looked as if it really had never been finished. Stairs were crude rails and stairs were just wooden steps. I don't think we ever had faculty meetings. He possibly had never heard of them. A pump was outside, and everyone had collapsible drinking cups. There was no sign of toilets. The boys went in the woods to one side of the building and the girls on the other. The children rode to school in covered wagons, which were farm wagons with benches on each side facing each other. The roads were dirt road, and, in the winter, there were four mules that had to pull the wagons.

Every child brought his lunch in a molasses bucket. When it was warm enough, they ate outside. But often, we brought a lunch and ate with them. I looked on in awe when they pulled these big biscuits out as large and as thick as a bun, purple! I knew exactly what they were eating. Their mothers took the hot white puffy biscuits out, put a big blob of butter on them, and then filled them with either blackberry jam or jelly. By the time they pulled them out to eat, they were purple because the hot biscuits had been shut up in the tin buckets. How did they eat them? They usually had sausage or ham too, and a piece of a cake or tea cake. I called them the "Purple biscuit eaters" only when I was at home.

There was a young man in the vicinity who had a good saddle horse and offered it to me to ride. This was about the best thing that had happened to me by that time. I had a pair of riding pants and boots and took a canter down the road several times.

One of my roommates, Effie, had a "regular" who came down for her almost every Friday to take her home, so they were certainly kind to let me have a ride. Julius Cruse was one of the wittiest people that I knew at that time. He kept us well entertained, and she married him later.

We. Effie and I became crossed up with our landlord. We had dates with two locals and stayed on the porch with them past ten o'clock and he read the riot act to us so we found another place to board with his brother.

Our room was combination guestroom and parlor. There was the old pump organ which Effie could play, a center table with a set of amber colored glasses and a pitcher on a tray. Our bed had the back of it almost reaching halfway to the twelve-foot ceiling. Over our bed was a large, and I mean large, photograph of a baby in a casket. This was very disturbing to us, but we dared not say anything because we supposed it was their child. Later on, I asked her if she had only the two girls and she told me she had not. Then I asked about the picture over the bed. Someone gave it to her and didn't know whose baby it was!

Mr. Gadford made our fire at four o'clock in the morning. Of course, he was fully dressed because he had to come across a wide-open hall. After the fire got going, he picked up his guitar and played until daylight in their side and then he went to the barn for chores.

Breakfast was pot boiled coffee, ham, sausage, or fatback, eggs, blackberry jelly or jam, and great big white two-story biscuits. I always ate biscuits with top and bottom browned and no fluff in the center. I know I behaved rudely when I took the innards out of my biscuits, but that I did.

In the spring, there was tornado watching by everyone. I would not go to the storm cellar at all, and they tried to pull me out almost. My bad case of claustrophobia was when I was young, and I hid during a hide and seek game in the storm pit that had an open door. The "seeker" sat on it and wound not let me out. My conniption fit was a big one.

Near the end of the six months, the School Board met with us to tell us the money had played out. It was just up to us teachers. The children needed the two months. If we stayed, the parents of the children would take care of us. Some would be willing for us to stay maybe two or three nights or maybe a week. That was the deal we agreed to. We got notes from parents inviting us on certain nights. Most of them were one-night stays and we were glad of that for many times we had to sleep with one of the daughters. They tried very hard to give their best accommodations. Those people, parents, and their children, were good people.

When I came home on weekends, Momma almost made me take my clothes off before I came in. But I didn't turn up with lice nor seven-day itch.

I was not re-elected the next year. One of the parents saw Papa and told him what a wonderful teacher I was. Papa asked him why I was not re-elected. He saw, "Well, the school board did not like it because she rode a horse on the open road astride with pants on."

We taught that year for eight months but were paid for only six months $65.00 per month. Board was fifteen dollars. Momma made my clothes. My sister May was so glad I got home. She said, "She's so crazy about all of those people. The only reason she didn't marry one of them was because he didn't ask her."

Pinedale Revisited:

I went back for the fiftieth anniversary of the school. The old building looked better and was used for a community center. The school had consolidated with Macedonia School, but the pupils I taught were there.

The picnic was on the grounds. These people have gone through better days. Beautiful homes, great farmers, I felt so good about it all and especially since so many had remembered me. We did a lot of reminiscing. The box suppers paid for a pipe running from the hand pump with several holes along the pipe so that it became a fountain all along the pipe. The only drawback was that someone had to man the pump.

Now box suppers were the method used for fund raising. Girls prepared foot that could be carried in a basket, usually sandwiches or biscuit and meats, cakes, and maybe homemade candy. Then the boxes were decorated up beautifully with flowers, ribbons, and bows. The auctioneer would raise a box and the young men would bid on them. Two boys who like the same girl had to go deep in their pockets.

Another form of recreation at night was the séance, walking on the table. A round table seemed the best kind. As many as could sit comfortably around the table participated. Hands were spread out to touching and there was much concentration. The table legs were supposed to rise up. We never got into the séance long enough to hear voices which I did not condone. But there was something about the hands touching that got those table legs off the floor so easily.

Everyone went to the Bethel Baptist Church on

Wednesday night prayer meeting. Miss Lindsey Gafford shouted, and it was a command performance. She would race up and down the aisle clapping and shouting. One little fourteen-year-old girl in my homeroom was attacked by her because she had not given her life to Jesus. She hovered over this girl and called on the Holy Ghost. The girl became hysterical, and Miss Lindsey shouted that Jesus had come into her heart. Never did I want so much to go to that poor little thing and take her from that woman. Thank goodness there are not many churches that have Miss Lindsey about or we all would turn in to infidels.

I saved enough money that year to go to summer school in Memphis and take education courses so I would not have to take that exam again. It was a nice eight weeks. During that time, Bill Steep, my first love from my freshman and sophomore years at MSCW was in dental school there. We had our first date. The last year in college in Columbus he was playing with the New York Giants. He got his knee injured and settled for dentistry. The date was a dinner dance at the nightclub in Memphis. That date fell as flat as a flounder. Maybe it was due to that fact that a country schoolteacher and someone who had been places did not work.

I dated a student at Memphis State Teachers College that summer. He had a job with the Park Commission in Memphis helping supervise playgrounds in the summer. My eight-week term was in late May. Our eight-month school term was over in April.

He encouraged me to apply and brought me forms to fill out. It was important to play a musical instrument. I told him I fooled around on the piano but could not play. He told me every playground had a piano, so don't put that down, but instead a cello for no one carried a cello. I lied on that form paper and thirty years later I had an opportunity to learn to play cello. My G string broke and too many things were happening for me to have it restrung, but I felt I have been absolved.

The fall following, I was able to get a job in the eastern part of the country, at Center School. It was five miles from New Albany. With no conveyance, teachers lived in the vicinity. Two other teachers and I rented two rooms from the principal next to school. It was unfurnished so we had to furnish it. The patrons had extra items which we rented. The double bed was $1.25 a month. Allene Baker and I used it. Ruth White slept on a cot which was fifty cents a month. The dresser was $2.00 even if the drawers didn't close. We each bought a chair from home. The oil stove was $1.50 a month. We used a card table I had brought from home for our table. We were five miles from New Albany and every night we went out to look at the glow from the lights in town. There was electricity in the house. A hydrant was in the yard. Our rent was $15.00 a month. I think this was the lowest living standards the three of us ever experienced. The principal was the worse. He had six hogs that wintered under the house and were all over the school ground. The patrons thought he was sent from God to them. His prayers every morning in the chapel were long and brought tears almost to the children's' eyes. We knew he was stealing from the school for he bought all kinds of things and used them for himself.

Our one getting away from it all was walking through the woods four miles to Wallerville every day for our mail and our buying a bar of candy and having a nice visit with postmistress. One of the high school students cut us a staff and we used that to help us along and sometimes went back to our childish ways and pretended they were our horses.

I taught biology without any kind of lab. I found a big bottle on the shelf for our so-called lab. It had no label on it, so I opened it to see what it smelled like. One big whiff and I was on the floor—OUT! The boys got me up and they fanned me, opened the door and in a second, I came to my feet. No more opening unlabeled bottles for me.

My homeroom was of third, fourth and fifth grades. They sat in those double desks which were discards from possibly the schools in New Albany. I noticed particularly one little boy who had lesions all over his hands and he was forever scratching them. Then other pupils appeared with the same problem. We had a new doctor at the Health Department, so I called him, and he came out. After examining all the class, he announced to me that it was Eczema, which in common language is Seven Years Itch. He also advised me to buy Lysol and disinfect all books, pencils, even erasers and to wipe off the desks. We scrubbed everything. Parents were notified.

A few days later I went home because I had the same thing. Dr. Wesson diagnosed and gave me a prescription. Mama disregarded that prescription and had me completely covered with sulfur and lard. I was confined in one room with a pair of outing pajamas on. It was certainly quarantine. Food was brought to me on a tray and for three days, this was my treatment, salving me down with the treatment. The itch was gone, and I was back in school. It had cleared up, but I was very careful not to pick up anyone's pencils, books, or their assignments on papers even. It did finally go away.

But the doctor came back, and all was clear. He asked if he could talk to me outside the door. I obliged and he asked me for a date on Friday night. It was great to be picked on Friday nights and get to spend the weekend at home, with a date on Sunday night and then be taken back to Center School. A great break. This gentleman was attentive for the next two years of my life! Dr. Irvin Trapp was a Mississippian who had just come back from New York.

The Trustees approached the sixth month to tell us the money had played out. Of course, we agreed to stay on the eight months. The last three weeks I picked up the flu germ. Papa came for me, and he was alarmed about my living conditions. I think he must have given the principal some harsh words. He took me home and told him I would not be coming back.

Summer came and went. I was given a rush by Irvin Trapp. Papa liked him and I'm sure he thought he was a "great catch." We never got that far. I was not attracted to him at all. He had a Buick sports car, and we went to ever kind of cultural thing that came to Memphis. I was polite.

A job at the Ritz Theater in New Albany opened up and I took it. I worked in the ticket office. After the second show began, I could leave so I had a date nearly every night. Boring and I had a guilt complex about it. I finally made arrangements with my sister Ruby and Nisbet and stayed with them. Nisbet liked movies so he came with me and walked me home, so I only dated Irvin on weekends.

I taught the next year in Center but four of us commuted. Mariela Sanford, Mildred Rogers, Audrey Randle, and I rode in Mariela's Ford Coupe. I had to sit on Aubrey's fat lap. Things were better. I was still living with Ruby and Nisbet. They had three children by now: John, Jean, and Betty. We all three slept in the same room. Nisbet was working at the compress then, on a very meager salary. I don't know how they managed to keep Florence, but they did. Maybe my rent went to pay her. She was a treasure and a wonderful cook, but so was Ruby.

There are some really funny incidents that happened during the time when I was dating Dr. Trapp. I think they merit writing. Irvin's sister, Neva, was in MSCW when I was there, and she taught music at the Ashland School in Benton County. Benton was a county bordering Un-ion my home county. He usually picked her up as we went to Memphis to different programs.

This particular night, we had gone to a play in Memphis. We always stopped afterwards for a late meal. Thus, we were on our way. Neva and I were asleep. The car slowed down and we heard this from Irvin, "What do I see?" Coming toward us on the roadside there three huge animals, one behind the other. Our car was barely moving. As we approached them, we all yelled, "Elephants!" There were three men walking beside them. This was a gravel country road halfway between Ashland and Holly Springs. Neva very slowly said that she remembered there was a circus advertised in Ashland. There was no railroad in Ashland, and they were walking the elephants back to Holly Springs where they would join the circus. The article in the Memphis Commercial Appeal wrote the story of us stating Dr. Irvin Trapp had seen elephants that were not pink.

I had not dated anyone for two years. The athletic director and teacher in the high school was his friend. There was a chance occasion when I was thrown with him. The chemistry was right. He took me home. I had dates with him. I had such a good time with him. We hit it off just right. This was just about to develop into a romance. Then one night when we were not seeing each other, Irvin appeared at the window to tell me it was important he see me when I was ready to leave.

He was there and I went with them. We drove out to a churchyard at the Ebenezer Church near Cotton Plant. He gave me such a tongue lashing, how I had betrayed him and influenced his best friend, on and on. I tried to tell him he had no hold on me, so take me home and I would not see him again. No way would that romance ever bud. George came the last time, and he was glad I found out. He could not date his good friend's girl that he expected to marry. That took care of our seeing him again. So, I started dating some of the local boys who were my friends. Louise Mack and I had fun and no "ties" attached to it.

My next year of teaching was at Calhoun City, circa fifty miles from home. A friend, Ethel McCurry, had taught there some years before. She took Mildred and me down and we got the jobs, mine in fifth grade, and hers in sixth. We found a very nice place to board. Our landlady was from old stock Calhoun City, so we were immediately introduced to the "right people."

Because I had more experience, my salary was $48.00 a month. Mildred's was $45.00. This was a very pleasant place to live, running water, a flushing toilet and the landlady was a good cook. Two of our meals were with her. Board was $25.00 a month, over half our salary.

Her father and mother came for a visit. He became critically ill, so much, that we were farmed out to the Methodist minister and his wife. They were both very cordial and much younger. Mildred and I were singing in the choir at church. It was a tossup: teach Sunday School or sing in the choir. We chose the choir. Mildred had had voice lessons her four years at MSCW and had a beautiful voice, so she became the soloist.

We were paid the first two months, and then given a pink slip to hold until the last month of school. Bingo! Our landlady could not keep us with such an arrangement so out we went, hunting a roof over our heads.

A new family moved into town. There were the McKewens, and their daughter Margaret was in my fifth-grade class. They rented a big barnlike house. When they heard of our problem, the opened up their home. They let two rooms out to us, their dining room and bedroom joining it. The rooms were large and seemed adequate to us. There were the three of us, Ann Eliza Scott, Mildred, and me. We had a double bed and a twin bed. Linens were furnished. Our dining room had their dining room furniture in it, and we had the oil stove to cook on. This was rented to us for $7.00 each and we would not pay until we received our checks at the end of the school year. Can you think anyone every so kind and trusting as these people!

Every weekend our dates would bring us quail, squirrels, and doves. Sometimes the mothers would cook them and send them over. Patrons would send chicken and dressing and cakes every weekend. We ate our mid date meal at the restaurant in town. It was wonderful food and only $.25 per meal.

These two people were avid bridge players. Every night enough people would drop in to have two tables. Then the townspeople had us for bridge and dinner. We were well cared for. There were social activities there more than any place I've seen, even after the lean days of the Depression were over.

Calhoun City was a little town of about 1500 people. Everyone was accepted, a remarkable little town. Dates were different from anywhere. One night, one of the young men who I or one of the others had a date with might call for a date and we were all together with maybe one or two nights a week going to a movie or playing bridge. We were friends with many of the girls in town and we were invited to bridge and dinners in their homes.

The first few months of school I had a fleeting romance with the coach, Walter Patty. I thought the sun would not rise or set if he did not call. He was fun, handsome and had all the qualities I expected to find in a young man. Every morning, he waited to walk to school with me. I was certainly pleased. One morning as we came to the cracks in the walk, we were chanting, "Step on a crack and you break your grandma's back." Suddenly the cracks began to appear with "pussy" written on every one of them. I was so red-faced, and I thought he was laughing on the inside at this.

That afternoon when I took the fifth grade for their twenty-minute play period, three of the boys had to stay in to finish an assignment that was past due. On our return, written across the floor in big letters with chalk was the word, "pussy." I asked the three boys to stay after school. Then I wrote the word "pussy" on the board and asked them to get out their dictionaries and find the definition of the word which they did. So, I asked them to write each word and come to the board and write the definitions. After they had to write it five times at their seats. Well, done. The next morning Walter and I walked to school without a chant, for behold, at every crack, was written, "pussy cat!" After dating Walter went on for some time, he did not play bridge and I saw him less and less.

Mildred's one love, Cecil Frazier managed Bower's Grocery Store in New Albany. He wrote that he would being us groceries but had no car. He talked Irvin Trapp in to calling me for a Sunday night dinner date. We needed groceries, but I did not need him, but finally gave him an answer. Let him come. They came. Cecil brought sacks full. When we were nearly out of food, they came back again and again, but with little encouragement from me. He wrote letters saying if I would give him a chance to express himself to me, there would be roses on Valentine's Day.

The last trip, I had two dollars left from five that my brother sent me. We were at the restaurant one lunch period when a man came in with two of the most beautiful balls of puff, Eskimo Spitz puppies. It was near my favorite niece Jean Grace's eighth birthday, so I paid my last two dollars for the puppy. We took her home with us. It cried at night. Mildred had already given a long lecture about frivolous spending and would not allow the puppy, which we named Bertha Ophelia, in our bed. Bless Eliza, she took Bertha as a bedfellow. We wondered how we would get Bertha home for the birthday. Well, the dear doctor had written for a date, so bingo, he and Cecil came with groceries on a Sunday afternoon. Springing Bertha on him was pretty awkward. We had to put her in a box. She was laid in swaddling clothing in the trunk. When I heard from Jean and her mother, my sister, Ruby, Dr. Trapp had put the dog out on the porch. I think they heard her and brought her in for the night. She lived a happy life and had six litters of puppies that sold for ten dollars apiece. The last time I saw my friend again was a dance after I was already engaged to Tread. I hope God has forgiven me for using him. He should have known what "no" meant or I showed that I was not interested.

School went on. Mildred and I found rides home, then we had to come back with the paper man who left New Albany at 3:30 in the morning. We would catch him and ride in the cab with him. He was a man of questionable character, but he didn't show that side to us. We would fold his papers and help him throw them out. The sun had just come up and it was early springtime with big wild violets in full bloom. We marveled over them so much that he said, "I'm just going to have to let you young ladies get out and pick some."

We got into town to find out Franklin Delano Roosevelt had closed all the banks. Of course, it was no bother to us since we didn't have any money anyway. I had bought a maroon crepe dress for $1.89. That was my Sunday dress. The reason it was marked down from $3.00 was because it had a gash in the shoulder. I sewed it up and it had a berth like lace collar that covered my stitches. Then Mama made clothes for me, so I got by.

We had a fireplace in our bedroom. In late March, the wood was nearly gone. We had dates and when we drove anywhere and saw a stick of weed, it was put in the trunk and used. Finally, our dates would grab a piece here and there. That Depression left its mark on me. Every time I see a stick of wood on the roadside, it's very hard for me not to stop and pick it up.

I was basketball coach for the girls. That's not anything I would advise anyone to do. The bad things were girls playing rough, referees not calling games honesty, trip away from home base. My girls were perfect. They were such a sweet lot of young ladies. I enjoyed them, but it was a rough game and those little towns around were hot for their own teams. Basketball season was over before Spring.

We bade Calhoun City goodbye rather tearfully, especially the people we lived with, who were so caring and full of fun and the young people our age who had provided us with much of our social life. It was a good year. Our sense of values, except for my lost two dollars spent for a puppy. We bade them all goodbye, declaring we would return.

I had a few shekels left over after late board to McKewens were paid, so new ideas and plans sprang forth. When I went to college, I wanted to major in Physical Education. But to my dismay, they had dropped that major because there was no demand or there were too many majors from college. I was very good in all of the classes of Physical Education. Miss Pohl was well known everywhere in Mississippi and many other places, was the head of the department with five others in the department. I went out for every sport, except basketball! I was accepted in her special dancing class and Miss Pohl knew me. So, I wrote her in early summer and asked where I could find a college for a Physical Education major. She gave me the name of the American College of Physical Education in Chicago. So, after writing to them for all information and then to her to send my credits and a letter of recommendation, I was accepted and given a plan to help me financially. All of my MSCW credits were accepted, and I could get my degree at the end of the year, being 1934.

Plans were made with lukewarm approval from my parents and siblings. One of the offers in financial ad was finding me a place to without paying board. This sounded good to me.

A big culture shock—I was off to Chicago by train. Someone from the college was there to meet me which was a relief. And on to the college via the El which I had never seen or heard of, riding up high over the big city was strictly an eye opener to me. But I remembered that you don't get awed by everything you see so I pretended it was old hat and arrived calmly. Being classified as a senior, I would have to teach under classes, Swedish, Gymnastics, German Gymnastics, Diving, and all kinds of swimming lessons. I certainly gave all these ponderings in my heart. I had never heard of Swedish and

German.

Gymnastics and the only diving I ever did was jumping off the pier at Hall Neely's Lake holding my nose. Oh wow! I was plenty awed by all this.

Then I inquired of living accommodations. The young lady who met me took me to one or two of the settlement houses that I thought about Jones Adams type. There was no way I would have lived in one of those. At the present, all new students were staying in the dormitory like place until accommodations were found.

One day I saw on the bulletin board, AuPair, which meant living as a member of a family with special household duties and speaking French was required. The number was called, and the French woman was understood to say she would like for me to come for an interview. I did not speak French which was explained to her.

I was taken out at the appointed time. It was in Northern Chicago, but we made it shortly without having to transfer.

She was certainly French without opening her mouth, very petite, blonde, very attractive, the flat very lovely with good taste and not fussy. After some conversation, the setup, an American husband, three children, one twelve-year-old boy named John, a seven-year-old daughter named Denise, and a three-year-old named George Pierre. My duties were to take the children to the beach, Lake Michigan, every afternoon. I would put George Pierre in the stroller and help the other children with their homework, and then bathe, feed, and put George Pierre to bed. I would dine with them, have a private room, and assist her with the kitchen. That did not sound too bad since I didn't have any schoolwork except bone up on German and those many gymnastics. I would practice doing them in my free time.

The location of this college was on Diversity Street, the heart of the Mafia headquarters. This was 1933, remember, and the crime was at its peak. I did not know this until later. There's nothing like trust.

There had been a Dr. Weinkoff in Chicago who had performed an operation on her daughter in law. The patient died during the operation and the mother-in-law was held responsible. I was at the fair on a Saturday and rode the Skyline Drive over the lake. After I was on, one of the passengers whispered, "Do you know the person operating this is the husband of the woman his mother is accused of killing?" I began to be more cautious. Mr. Howard of my home in Chicago warned me to be on the alert in my goings and comings.

Back to college. My tank suit for swimming had not arrived so I sat by the pool with the others watching the dive class. The instructor stood by the side of the diving board with a big stick. He was a huge man. If the diver did not spring off when he gave the signal a tap on the legs was given.

I learned to swim at Hall Neeley's, a few miles down the road from home. The only diving I did was to jump off the pier holding my nose. I was scared within an inch of my life.

I went to the college doctor and told him I had serous sinus problems and in no way could I dive. That took care of my diving class. I had swimming lessons at MSCW, so I dropped back to the intermediate class. I was in the special dancing class taught by Emma Ody Pohl, but the dancing class was ballet. That was not too bad. No toe dancing. I had dropped back so many times the registrar called me in to tell me it would take another year for me to graduate. I began to expect this earlier.

I found out in a short time that this was not the kind of PE I expected to teach. All the students looked and acted as if being in the Olympics was their goal. One of the students had swum Lake Michigan at one of its narrow locations and she was working hard to do the English Channel. They were all seasoned athletes. One student from Dallas, Dorothy Baird, became my only close friend. She was a new one and had come to the school for the same reason I had.

When I talked to the registrar, I told her I did not have the money for another year, and they found all kinds of ways to keep me and Dorothy. We could go to school and pay later. We knew this was not our cup of tea. So, we went on until we finished the first quarter in late November.

Mr. Howard was so relieved for he worried about me. Renee Howard, his wife, and I had grown to be good friends, maybe because I could communicate with her better than those fast-talking Chicago people. The Weinkoff trial was coming up and I asked her if we could go and hear it. We set the date. Kenneth, Mr. Howard, told us to take notebooks and be students from our Criminology Class so we started out. At the courthouse, I had to do all the talking and asked where the Weinkoff trial would be. It had been postponed because the doctor was ill. So, since we were students from Criminology Class, where was another trail they would recommend.

They took us in the courtroom where there was a bug murder case taking place, ushered us to the front seats among very official looking persons. We sat with our notebooks open. Of course, her notes were taken in French. The only thing I knew to do was to take mine in Pig Latin. We heard whispers of "reporters." We left at the next break and forgot about the Weinkoffs.

Renee was very ambitious and wanted to start a private kindergarten and call it the French American Kindergarten. Her ambition finally was becoming a reality. French was spoken at the table, so my French was just little polite sayings. I would go out soliciting. She had gathered all the names in that part of Chicago. Our location was a half block from Evanston city limits. Out I went through the streets with list and ringing doorbells. She telephoned some and I went at ap-pointed times. It was quite interesting for most of the wives were French who had met American soldiers while stationed in France during World War I.

Their English I could figure out when the accent was always different from theirs. They were all anxious that their children could not learn their native tongue. Renee had found some kind of off brand church that would rent the Sunday School rooms during the week. There was a small but adequate play area. Twenty pupils were all that she could take. Before we could plan too far, I had to go to the Cook County Superintendent's office to get a permit to open such. My credentials had to be sent for. She supplied hers as well as citizenship papers and a few other requirements.

We were ready to start on December first. I wrote my sister Ruby back home to make two short smocks for us from the same fabric. They came and we wore those. They had big bows that went to the bottom of the smocks.

My job was to greet them all nine each morning, help them remove their wraps, and teach them to hand them, place their shoes on a shelf where their house shoes were and put them on. French lessons were started for five in a class while I did artsy, crafty things with the others. Children's art is the best. They are so creative and free.

I took care of their play outside, then followed by juice and cookies. The French was taught in small groups but there was singing by all. Renee played and sang beautifully. The school was dismissed at noon when the mothers came for them, and each child took home his "show and tell."

The afternoon left me free time. I spend much time in the downtown library. There was a young man who was in one of the sections. I met him and each time I came he'd ask me to go for coffee at his break. He was David Davidson. He always found new books and recommended these to me. He invited me to go to hear the Chicago Philharmonic. Before he got my answer, he prefaced it with, "Do you mind being seen with a Jew?" and my answer was, "Why should I mind?" We went out several more times. They were usually on Sunday afternoons for I had to meet him there. I'm sure he had no automobile. The Howards seemed to frown on this, but I met new people and didn't get back to the library very often. I enjoyed his company. He was a gentleman, very refined and loved music.

Back in the hometown, New Albany, the sister of my dear friend Louise Owen, wrote to me. She had gone to the University of Illinois in Champlain and had a good friend who she still kept up with, so she sent her name, address, and telephone number. She had married since Mamie had last seen her, but she sent me her name, address, and telephone number.

This was great news for me. I called. They lived in a flat, Southside Chicago, near the University of Chicago, where her husband George was still in school. Would I please come to dinner on a date at 7:00 p.m.? This was to be a great event for me. I dressed in my best, high heels, and all. This is December in Chicago and why I forgot to wear galoshes, I will never know. With my directions and a dollar in my pocketbook, I took to El to South Chicago. You see a lot of Chicago that you'd rather not see on an El. I got to my El destination at 6:30. The address was a block away. I could not arrive early, and I was freezing by the time I got to a corner drugstore. I went in and stood by the radiator and of course, a clerk came over. What would I do? Well, five or six years ago, the Ouija Board was the thing to have because it told you quasi where you've been, where you are going and with who. This year it was not the item to have, and I assumed they would be out. So, I would just ask for one of those and get warm as well as waiting until time for me to arrive.

After I had asked for it, I was filled with all kinds of trepidations. What if he finds one? I have only one dollar. I can't say it's the wrong color or the wrong size. He came back saying they were out, but he would go back and look in stock. I don't know why I didn't just run out. He came back with "we don't seem to have any." I said I was sorry and thanked him for looking. I had warmed up then.

I arrived a few minutes socially late and glowingly warm. Ethel and George Kenyon were great people. We hit it off right away. She had finished the class with Mamie, my friend. It was a wonderful evening, and they had my telephone number and would call later. George was a trombone player with a band made of up of young men. They were a dance band playing about Chicago.

The next time I got to see them was out at a tea dance on a Saturday afternoon at the Palmer House. I was introduced to the band and during the afternoon, different members of the band would dance with Ethel and me. One came over and his face was so familiar, a very handsome young man. He told me he was a model for Arrow Shirts, so I began to find him in magazines, etc.

It was nearing Christmas and the little church we were renting for the kindergarten asked us if we could do the Christmas Story for them. We did oblige and used all the family in the production. Kenneth, the father, was Joseph, I was Mary, a doll was Jesus, John and Denise were shepherds, and George Pierre was the angel. Renee played the piano, and the children of the church sang.

In the meantime, George Kenyon's family had telephoned me and invited me to Christmas dinner with the family. It was a sumptuous affair, with 26 people at one table. Mrs. Kenyon's brothers and sister, Dr. Kenyon's two sisters, cousins galore, and George's sister and her husband were there. The far was the usual with turkey and fixings, but with boiled buttered onions, turnips, carrots, and two kinds of potatoes. They said it was tradition not to have the root vegetables which were available. It was a beautiful day and of course, they had a lovely gift for me. George's father was a dentist.

The Kenyon's were Episcopalians. I grew up Methodist. In my church in New Albany, they used the ritual in front of the book. It was the same as the Church of England. The Wesley's held on to that. We had kneeling pads and we knelt for prayers. This was a beautiful little church with a nice tall steeple. The sanctuary was right below the steeple and the pews were semi-circled with broad aisles with green runners. The aisles led to the sanctuary with the choir behind the place for the ministers, pulpit, and such.

Dick Hall was a Methodist with money. This was a time when Catholicism was a Satan descending people. That ritual sounded too Catholic. He maneuvered and had a big brick church built. No more ritual. I was so glad that I had become a member of the old one and it never went away. I went to the Episcopal Church in Columbus when the Rector was Duncan Montgomery Gray, who later became Bishop of Mississippi. Their rector was Fr. White. He always called me "Miss Ippi." Their home was always open to the Kenyon's, so I was with them and was a guest too. He inquired about the church in New Albany, and I said that there was none. He looked it up and told there was a service there once a month served by the Reverend James Butler from Holly Springs.

One Sunday I was invited by the Kenyon's to go to church with them and join them for Sunday dinner when the Reverend White and family would join them. I did not take money with me which was usually a dollar bill for any little emergencies leaving a dime for El fare. At church when the offering was taken, I erred and gave my dollar. I did not leave until late in the afternoon with no money! I panicked. There was the same drugstore so I went in and asked the young clerk if I could sell him five three cent stamps. It was all I had, and I explained how foolish I had been. He would not take the stamps but put two dimes in my hand and said, "You may accidentally drop one." The very next time I was in there, I took him the two dimes.

I was with Kenyon's now quite a bit. After the first of the year, Renee was required to get another teacher with kindergarten qualifications, so I was mostly in and out, but serving as an au pair.

I was still helping with the kindergarten, darting back and forth to friends in South Chicago. George's mother was a member of a club of some kind, so Ethel and I were invited to this. We went to all the museums several times. One of the outstanding things of the World's Fair was getting to see and hear television for the first time. It was blurry but unbelievable. Marshall Fields was a great place to meander through, much like a museum itself. It covered a block. Often times, I would forget the entrance I came in, and would go out another and be lost. I learned early not to panic because there was a big stalwart policeman on every corner. I certainly did not talk like those Chicago people, and I noticed he always prolonged our conversation, but he was always jovial and helpful.

The Eighteenth Amendment was repealed on December 3, 1933. We were in the loop, and it was a sight to see. We were glad that Kenneth Howard was with Renee and me. That week, the American Veterans were having their annual meeting in Chicago at the Palmer Hotel. I had read of the location of the Mississippi delegation and of course, I went to their room. I left as quickly as I could, but it took longer than I wanted it to. A roomful of drunk men from any place is where you don't want to be.

After one of the dances, we were invited to one of the homes for cocktails. Gin was served. It certainly didn't taste good, but I must have finished the drink. I have never been so sick. I was at Ethel's and George's. Ethel had to sit with me practically all the night. I've never touched gin again. The smell can turn me away even.

New Year's Eve was another wild time. All the doors were open up and down the halls and people wandered in and out. Everyone was pretty well inebriated who came and went. I had not had anything and was sitting reading a Shakespearian sonnet when a distinguished looking young man approached me. He was in very formal dress, tails and holding his top hat in hand. He said, "Y'all, hello, and what are you reading in this corner and disgustingly sober?" We exchanged little chit chat. He sat down and we visited for some time. During this time, he gave me his card and took my address and telephone number. Of course, I was impressed that this handsome person had assured me that he would call and hope that I would go to dinner with him.

He called a few days later and invited me to dinner and dance at the Drake Hotel. Renee had given me a very pretty blue knit dress. My sister Ruby had made me a snappy black velvet turban. Hats were worn when ladies went out in the evening, but no veils after six o'clock p.m.

He called for me in a Buick Coupe, smartly dressed, of course. The hotel at night was gorgeous with a floorshow, all so glamorous. The waiter brought the booze card. I had no earthly idea what to order. I knew for sure it wouldn't begin. An Old Fashioned sounded less wicked, so that was my order. The first swallow practically took the skin off my throat. That drink lasted me the whole night. Thank goodness, I had no ill effects, and we danced a lot. He was a wonderful dancer and I know I was good for I had been told by all my partners! The dinner was the best. We got home at a late hour. He saw me to the door with no advances, only clasping my hand in his for a minute and promising to call me in a day or two.

David Vandermeter did call, and I went out with him several more times. I never asked him what he did or where he worked. Ethel guessed that he was a professional gambler. I could not believe that.

In the meantime, my family found out that I was not in school, and I was not working at the school, the French American Kindergarten. The school had taken on so many children that Renee had to employ a teacher with a degree in order to keep it open. I was still with them though in the home.

I had a telegram from my sisters saying there was a job available, and I must be there within a few days. I had to get ready to say goodbyes. David came to put me on the bus. It was a sad farewell, he kissed me, our first kiss and I was off down South. I had to go by bus because they had sent me a bus ticket. It took me a while to get over my tears.

We exchanged two or three letters and that was the end of an almost romance. All of it had been a most memorable time with an interesting person.

I had letters from the Kenyon's many times and with Renee and Kenneth Howard. The Howards and I had renewed friendships later on.

And in Chicago, in Al Capone's era, I didn't get robbed. I did get drink on gin after the Repeal, no propositions, but I did find hospitality in the huge city of sin and corruption in which I never chanced to have bad experiences.

Appendix D: Josie's Reunion Letter to Classmates

CLASS OF '36

May 10, 1996

Ms. Sara White Underwood
1328 CR86
New Albany, MS 38652

Dear Class Member,

Can you believe I've heard from everybody!! ... And only one person (Broox Sledge) won't be able to join us. The program for our reunion weekend is as follows:

Saturday, June 8th:
11A	Registration at Park on the River (Behind Fred's store on Main Street - just follow the road)
12N	Picnic lunch
4:30 - 5:30P	Reception for former students and friends of class (401 Cleveland Street - Joan's home)
6P	Dinner for Class of '36 and their guests (401 Cleveland Street - Joan's home)

Sunday, June 9th:
10:45A	Service at First Methodist Church (Reserve seats for Class of '36 and guests)
12N	Dutch treat lunch at Oaks Country Club

You can either mail your check in advance or pay $23 per member and $23 for each guest when you arrive. (This fee includes food, Park Pavillion Rental, Memorial Flowers for church, etc. Please note that the lunch on Sunday is Dutch treat.) If you would like to mail a check, mail it to: Joan Morris, 401 Cleveland Street or Bill Harwell at 619 Highland Street, New Albany, MS, 38652.

Do remember to bring any pictures, newspaper clippings, snapshots and memorabilia to help us jog some wonderful memories! Also, please bring some of your favorite receipes--they'll be featured in the Heritage Cookbook. This cookbook will also include pictures of interest, and we'll have our group picture in the cookbook. (It's to be sold to help pay for the Faulkner Museum in New Albany.)

We look forward to seeing you on June 8th!

Joan Morris and Bill Harwell

Appendix E: Susie Bell's Favorite Recipes

One of these was her famous "cush" (rhymes with push). Per Blanche, "This was usually a dish made in the winter, mostly after hog killing when fresh pork was available. In her notes, the following was the procedure and ingredients:

A passel of leftover cornbread which was kept in the warming "closet" above the stove—Shallots from the garden was chopped, sage was added, the broth from the pork which could have been spareribs or back bones or the feet. This was mixed together in the big iron skillet and after some cooking and stirring, two or three eggs beaten were added and cooking continued until it was the consistency of dressing. And it tasted very much like dressing, but it was definitely "cush" and it is a rare thing to find it in any cookbook and most people never heard of such. But William Faulkner had because he mentions it in one or two of his novels. (After all, he was born in New Albany.)

Another favorite was bread pudding from a collection of leftover biscuits soaked in milk until the right consistency with eggs, sugar cinnamon and a bit of nutmeg. This was placed in a pan and baked. "If there was to be company, raisins were added," recalled Blanche. Rice pudding belonged to the favorite list, "and a crock full of tea cakes could be found after school with a glass of milk."

The family grew almost all of its food. Sugar and flour were bought along with spices, salt, and pepper. Jake and Susie Belle did not raise turkeys, but always had a big, fresh ham.

There would always be a fat hen baked. When Mama served any kind of meat, she felt there should be some kind of tart jelly, which was always wild plum jelly. Sweet potato pudding was a Christmas specialty. Potatoes were ground through the meat grinder, then eggs, spices, sugar, and butter and baked in the oven. Sometimes raisins would be added.

My favorite meal was chicken and rice, butterbeans, hominy, black-eyed peas, cornbread, and homemade ice cream for dessert. Sopping the cornbread in the "pot liquor" (black-eyed pea broth) was an added treat. Another favorite was dewberry pie. I would pick and fill a large bowl from bushes that stretched from behind the house all the way to Highway 30, deliver them to her and she would commence, almost immediately, making the pie. After baking she would place it in a window on the side of the house and always admonish, "Don't you touch that pie just yet, it's cooling."

Appendix F: Suzie Belle Ferguson Eulogy

By

The Rev. Joe E. Morris

Psalm 21:4

On an occasion such as this, there is a difference between sadness and mourning. It is a natural feeling to be sad at the passing of a loved one. The Greek poet Homer likened death of a beloved to the falling of a tree on the horizon. That horizon will never be the same. Our hearts can be legitimately sad for that absence.

But it would border on selfishness for us to mourn today. For we cannot mourn the passing of a life that was filled with 105 rich years; we cannot grieve for one whose life spanned more than we shall ever know, who lived and witnessed more history than we shall ever read; we cannot lament for one who is the mother of a genealogy that stretches for four generations, each with their own accomplishments and contributions to this life; we simply cannot mourn that kind of life, whose good qualities ran as much in depth as her years did in breadth.

So, accepting our sadness, we salute her victory. We pay homage to her triumph. It reflects the best of fortitude, determination, independence of spirit and strength in us all.

Aunt May remarked to me on Saturday: "This is no time to celebrate death, but a time to celebrate life." So, we shall: "He asked thee of life and thou gavest it him, even length of days forever and ever."

Faulkner wrote of his favorite character in his greatest

novel, one who personified strength, determination, and fortitude. He simply said, "She endured.'

Suzie Belle Lamar Ferguson endured.

Acknowledgements

This book is not just the story of one life, but of several. Apart from my own memory, I have relied upon the memories of others, on letters, journals, family papers and all else I could find. I relied heavily upon my brother, Dr. David M. Morris, CEO of Morris & McDaniel, International Consultant of Public Safety, particularly for documentation of dates and time frames, sequence of events, names of places and people. He also provided some of the photos.

Information on the history of New Albany and of Union County, Mississippi, was obtained from *Union County History* (Curtis Media Corporation, 1990) and the city's sesquicentennial archives. Jill Smith, Director of the Union County Historical Society and Museum provided invaluable insights. Lynn West, of the *New Albany Gazette,* diligently searched the paper's archives for news stories and other items of interest about Joan "Josie" Ferguson Morris as well as information about New Albany and Union County in the 40's, 50's and 60's.

Without the help and genealogical archives of Butch Gray, much of the family tree information would be missing. I also had genealogical data from mother's oldest brother, Guy Ferguson, he had accumulated from cemeteries across the country and from Scotland and the Register House in Edinburgh. Other family members making contributions were Allison Aldrich Jones (about her mother Blanche Ferguson Aldrich), Belle Jones Morgan (about her grandmother Blanche), Julie Renicker Riffel (about her mother Martha Glynn Ferguson Renicker), Liz Ferguson (about her grandfather Dan Ferguson), and Guy Ferguson (about his father Bill and grandfather Guy Ferguson.)

Sissy Bullock, Director of the Union County Anna Belle Stephens Memorial Library, helped recover old photos and documents. Jane Underwood Wiederman, in conjunction with the Union County Library produced a number of documents and photos relevant to the times, the people and events of that era.

I am grateful to Jeff Slagel, Librarian at Delta State University, and Lizzy Woodard, DSU Alumni official, along with Anna Sledge of DSU for their help in pinpointing Josie's year at that school and her activities. Equally helpful, providing the same from Hinds Community College, was Oliva Posey with that school's Alumni Association. Blue Mountain College personnel assisted in confirming the Interior Decorating course Josie audited.

Invaluable to this memoir are the multiple stories percolating the narrative. For those colorful and descriptive tales, readers can thank Jimmie Rogers, Margaret McGill Lane, Anne and Joe "Jo Jo" Wilkins III, Bill and Gayle Rutledge, Swift Rogers, Sandra Baker Moore, Patrice Parks, Ann Stephens, Gloria Wicker Cooper, Dr. David White, and others I may have missed.

The production of this book could not have occurred without the diligent and perceptive editing of my wife, Sandi, and author friend, Michael Hartnett. Both went the extra mile to insure a minimum of errors, both textual and grammatical and a smooth narrative.

I am deeply grateful to Nicole Mangum, CEO of Liberation's Publishing, for her willingness to take on the project, her love of the story and her dedication to its completion in a timely fashion.

The completion of this project has taken almost twenty

years, if one can imagine a memoir on my mother being *complete*. As you may have discovered, "Josie" Ferguson Morris is not an easy person to wrap your mind around.

www.ingramcontent.com/pod-product-compliance
Lightning Source LLC
Chambersburg PA
CBHW071959110526
44592CB00012B/1149